HEADING
HOME
WITH
JESUS

Debbie Philip blends the hues of lengthy personal experience in ministry among Chinese students, in-depth research, more than 100 visits to returnees in China, relevant Biblical passages, wise and gentle recommendations, and articulate descriptions of a multi-faceted framework in presenting rich and unique portraits of the realities and challenges, as well as the necessary preparations that Chinese believers studying abroad should consider. The portraits include both a composite "generic" Chinese student reflecting the Chinese contexts, and seven real Chinese student stories. This gift is equally valuable for host-country friends of the Chinese academic community who wish to help with reentry preparation. Non-Chinese readers will appreciate a readable and succinct overview about the various Chinese contexts and culture. This treasure is for all—Chinese and everyone else.

Leiton Edward Chinn, MA
former Lausanne Catalyst for International Student Ministries and former president of the Association of Christians Ministering among Internationals (ACMI)

Dr. Debbie Philip's book is an invaluable addition to the body of literature on Chinese returnees. The stories from her research shed light on the important issues and concerns that International Student Ministry (ISM) workers need to know and address in order to provide the best assistance to returning Chinese graduates and scholars. By painting the historical and cultural contexts that the students are coming from and returning to, readers have a fuller appreciation of the specific challenges Chinese returnees face. I am impressed with Dr. Philip's humble recognition of the need for global partnership among churches, ministries and organizations in providing a more complete reentry service. This book is a testament to the power of the Gospel to change international student lives. It is a must-read book.

Lisa Espineli Chinn, MA
pioneer in the area of international student reentry and served as the national director of International Student Ministry Department of InterVarsity/USA.

We live in an exciting time! More and more students go abroad to do (part of their) studies there; Europe being the number one destination at the moment. This gives us amazing opportunities to reach them with the gospel. Many Chinese students are very open to connect with local Christians and learn more about Christianity. Some of them come to faith in Christ. But how can we help them when they return to their home country which is so different? Debbie D. Philip has done extensive research in this field and has now written a very helpful and practical book. I highly recommend it to anyone who is involved in ministry and encounters Chinese students.

Francina de Pater, PhD
IFES International Student Ministry coordinator for Netherlands and Europe

Philip's knowledge of China and its people shines a light on the cultural factors that create dissonance for Chinese returnees. Her in-depth interviews with returnees, including stories of both thriving and waning faith, richly illustrate the challenges that Chinese returnees face. Philip provides cogent analysis of those interviews, as well as very practical suggestions to help Chinese return home well. This book will enable the reader to reach Chinese international students with the greater goal in mind: to see Chinese returnees successfully transplanted back to China, thriving in their faith and serving the Chinese church.

Benjamin Stevens
cross-cultural worker, East Asia

HEADING HOME WITH JESUS

Preparing Chinese Students to Follow Christ in China

DEBBIE D. PHILIP

WILLIAM CAREY
LIBRARY

www.missionbooks.org

Published by William Carey Library, an imprint of William Carey Publishing
10 W. Dry Creek Cir | Littleton, CO 80120 | www.missionbooks.org

William Carey Publishing is a ministry of Frontier Ventures
1605 E. Elizabeth St | Pasadena, CA 91104 | www.frontierventures.org

Andrew Sloan, copyeditor
Mike Riester, cover design
Koe Pahlka, Mike Riester, interior design

Printed in the United States of America
22 21 20 19 18   5 4 3 2 1 BP500

Library of Congress Cataloging-in-Publication Data

Names: Philip, Debbie D., author.
Title: Heading home with Jesus : preparing Chinese students to follow Christ in China / Debbie D. Philip.
Description: Littleton : William Carey Library Publishing, 2018. | Includes bibliographical references and index. |
Identifiers: LCCN 2018014271 (print) | LCCN 2018015775 (ebook) | ISBN 9780878080731 (mobi) | ISBN 9780878080748 (epub) | ISBN 9780878080724 (pbk. : alk. paper)
Subjects: LCSH: Christianity—China—20th century. | Christianity—China—21st century. | Church work with students. | Church work with foreign students.
Classification: LCC BR1288 (ebook) | LCC BR1288 .P45 2018 (print) | DDC 275.1/083--dc23
LC record available at https://lccn.loc.gov/2018014271

Acknowledgments

I am very grateful to the many returnees who gave so generously of their time, especially those who shared their stories as part of the formal research.

My thanks also go to friends and colleagues who read chapter drafts. Each one of you made very helpful comments. But don't worry, I take full responsibility for the final product!

Many people have prayed for this book, my work, and me over the past few years. Thank you for keeping me going. Some have given generously to support my financial needs too. May God bless you for your trust. My church has been constant and generous in prayer, encouragement, and financial support. I think they have also been unusual in supporting work which is neither traditional overseas work nor local work that primarily contributes to their own ministries.

Finally, thank you to our Lord, Jesus Christ, for his wonderful gift of salvation, hope, and purpose, and for the joy and privilege of meeting so many Chinese brothers and sisters.

Contents

Introduction

Chinese Students Abroad Returning Home

Take a stroll across any English-speaking university campus in North America, Australia, the UK, or elsewhere, and invariably you'll find that a large proportion of the students are internationals. More often than not, a high percentage of those students came from China. These students represent a twofold opportunity.

Chinese people value overseas qualifications highly and therefore work hard to achieve them. Increasingly, Chinese are studying in other languages too, for example, in the Netherlands, Germany and South Korea. In addition, many also enjoy practicing English, experiencing other cultures, connecting with friendly local people, and even seeking answers to deep questions. It is in these moments of connection that our first opportunity presents itself: the opportunity to be Christ's ambassadors to international students, letting them experience his love through us.

Chinese students are like other international students in that they are looking to make friends and experience a sense of belonging. They look for friendly people and for opportunities to investigate the host culture. Christians typically have a reputation for being kind; and, indeed, our love and warmth lead visiting students to join our church services, social activities, or even Bible study groups. Some come to such events for help in a crisis, experiencing peace as they listen to the singing. Others simply enjoy the security of being with caring strangers.

They appreciate developing friendships with local residents and other students, and they enjoy learning what Christians believe. For many, their religious interest remains purely theoretical, of cultural curiosity, or a means of making contacts. Some, however, come to the point of making a profession of faith—perhaps even being baptized—in the host country.

In recent years a steady stream of graduates has been returning to China after making some form of statement of faith in Christ. These returning students represent the second part of our twofold opportunity: they can share the love of Christ with others upon returning home.

After returning home, these new believers *should* be well placed to serve God in their country. That's the theory, at least. Unlike foreign missionaries, they don't need to spend years learning the language and culture.

But how much do we really know about what happens after they go home? Indeed, how much do we really know about what they believe? Imagine that student who has come to your church this year. When she returns home, will she settle in church, grow in faith, and contribute to God's kingdom in China? Or will she seem so promising, so excited about the answers to her prayers, so keen to be baptized, only to return home and quickly give up on church, Bible reading, prayer—and even on Jesus?

The Potential

Most mainland Chinese live in a materialistic, atheistic culture that values money, possessions, and status above all. With so many studying abroad—523,700 in 2015 alone[1]—and coming within range of the gospel, the potential contribution to the Chinese church and to extending Christian faith and values to the Chinese society is huge.

Estimates of the number of believers in China vary. Although conservative estimates number the Chinese church around seventy million,[2] even one hundred million Christians would still leave more than 1.2 billion people—over 92 percent of the population—without Christ. China has fifty-six ethnic minorities, speaking many different languages, and 516 people groups, of whom 83 percent are designated "unreached."[3] The opportunity is great. These returning students could be poised to start people movements toward Christ.

There is competition, of course, for the souls of the Chinese. While interest in Christianity has grown recently, so has interest in Buddhism and in traditional Chinese religious practices, such as temple worship and astrology. The desire for an ever more affluent lifestyle also entices many.

What Really Happens After Return?

In the past decade new believers have returned to China and contributed to the church and society in many ways, serving in churches and sharing the gospel with family members and others. Some are playing leading roles in church, combining that with busy secular jobs; others are focusing on serving Christ in their workplace, putting that service before career or material advancement. Unfortunately, however, Christians who work with international students have shared the sad news that many who professed faith abroad appear not to continue in their faith after returning home to China.

The parable of the sower (Luke 8:4–15) is apt here. Many seeds have fallen on the path, on rocky ground, and among thorns. Some have no real root or understanding, others are put off when the first challenges come their way, and others are distracted by life's worries, riches, and pleasures.

Two Contrasting Stories

Two young women provide a thought-provoking comparison. Xue and Ling[4] both went abroad in their twenties to get master's degrees. They were both single

---

1   "A Record Number of Chinese Students Abroad in 2015 but Growth Is Slowing," ICEF *Monitor*, April 6, 2016, http://monitor.icef.com /2016/04/ a- record- number- of-chinese- students- abroad-in-2015-but-growth-is-slowing/.

2   The Pew Forum 2011 Report on Global Christianity is often cited as a reliable, conservative estimate of the number of Christians in China. It reported sixty-seven million in 2010: fifty-eight million Protestants and nine million Catholics.

3   "Country Lists," Operation World website, http://www.operationworld.org/chna. Note that Operation World lists the number of Christians in China as well over one hundred million.

4   Returnees' names have been changed to avoid being identified.

at the time and the only child in their families. Each met Christian students who introduced them to social activities in which they met other Christians and got into discussions about what Christians believe. Both joined small groups with other international students, thus reading the Bible and learning about Christianity. Both made a statement of faith and were baptized. Both returned to their home cities and found jobs.

After returning, both Xue and Ling faced challenges to their commitment to follow Christ. Neither initially located a church that matched their idea of what a good church should be like. Xue's UK Christian friends put her in touch with a fellowship made up of returnees. Ling found no such group in her city. She visited a few house churches, but after a year she stopped going completely.

Both women's parents arranged dates for their daughters with eligible young men. Both Xue and Ling wanted to marry, but they wanted to marry a Christian—which their parents couldn't understand. What did Christianity have to do with marriage?

Ling's parents were also frustrated that she spent so much time on Sundays in church. Eventually Ling met a kind young man and they fell in love. They have been happily married for several years and now have a young son. Ling's husband is not a believer, and they don't go to church.

On the other hand, for ten years, Xue acquiesced to her parents' dating arrangements while maintaining her commitment to marry only a Christian. She became a church leader and has helped disciple many new believers. Later she married a Christian.

Xue and Ling's stories are told in more detail later in this book.

The Reason for This Book

It is no longer unusual to hear of mainland Chinese international students saying they have become Christians, or even have been baptized, abroad. But what do such apparent statements of faith mean? Have they really understood the gospel? And if they have, what changes in their lives reflect that understanding? In what ways do they think and act differently since they found Christ?

After all, when people truly turn to Christ and are born again their whole identity, purpose, and core values (what matters to them most) will change. But how will that play out in China, a context so different than when Chinese were living abroad? And what helps or hinders them from continuing to follow Christ back home?

My intent in this book is to answer these questions. The more we understand where people are coming from (mentally and emotionally as well as geographically) and what they are returning to, the more effectively we can relate to them while they are in our churches.

As in all cross-cultural communication, misunderstandings about what Chinese students believe or what we are conveying of the gospel will occur. However, if we understand better the Chinese context—so different from our own—that has shaped our Chinese friends and to which they will return, we can better help them prepare to flourish back home.

A specific goal of this book is that more of us can relate to Chinese students in ways that help them think through a biblical response to the challenges their faith will encounter in the mainland Chinese context, and how best to share the gospel in that context. A second goal is to help us, their host Christian brothers and sisters, identify which of the things we have been doing are helpful and which are less so and need to change.

Assumptions Made

A key assumption behind this book and the research which led to it is that *deciding to follow Christ involves fundamental personal change.* This assumption is made both on biblical and personal grounds. Paul discussed, in Colossians 3 and elsewhere, the concept of putting off the "old self" with its practices and putting on the "new self" in Christ.

I have experienced such change personally. Coming to faith in Christ forever affected how I spend my time and who I spend it with, as well as my attitudes toward work, money, and relationships. Both my daily motivations and what I consider my ultimate purpose on this planet have been shaped by my knowing, loving, and following Christ. In fact, the assumption of this book is that following Christ equates to a paradigm shift in what I believe to be the nature and direction of the universe, how I came to be included in it, and who made me. It encompasses a change in worldview and of the story, or narrative, I hold in my head about who I am. Going even one step further, I am convinced that these changes are not entirely of my own making; somebody else is involved—and that somebody is God.

Though these changes in my life are real, they did not all happen instantly. So what about the mainland Chinese who profess faith in Christ in their host country and then return to China, to a very different culture? If people are born again, they will change; but not all changes will occur immediately. I decided to investigate whether and how what mattered to individuals most (their core values) changed after they made a profession of faith in Christ while studying abroad. The most practical way to do that was to ask people who had been back in China for at least one year to tell me about their lives, from childhood until the present day.

Although what I found will not be true of every mainland Chinese returnee, my interviews and visits with more than a hundred returnees, plus the comments of other Chinese and foreign Christians I have spoken with, suggest that the issues and experiences described in this book have much wider application.[5]

---

5   The formal interviews were conducted as part of a PhD program. My PhD research greatly informed the contents and shape of this book.

The Contents of This Book[6]

This book offers five things:

- **A picture, or diagram**—to aid understanding of what happens when someone professes faith in one culture and then returns home to a different culture;

- **Information**—about the mainland Chinese context and its effect on students arriving from and returning to China;

- **Seven stories**—of individual returnees;

- **Explanation**—of ideas in the diagram and what needs to change if someone is to continue following Christ back home;

- **Suggestions**—on how to help people prepare to return.

The stories illustrate challenges and opportunities encountered by Chinese returnees. They also illustrate the concepts in the diagram.

The ideas behind the diagram helped me understand what has been happening to Xue, Ling, and other returnees I know in China. I hope it will help you as well.

The Purpose and Readership of This Book

There is no doubt that the emerging powerful China we now know will wield immense influence in years to come. The question is *What kind of influence will that be?* We want returning students, China's academic and economic elite, to contribute to God's kingdom as part of China's future influence. We want these returnees to take root in Christ and persevere in times of testing. And rather than being choked or distracted by the expectations of twenty-first century Chinese life, we want them to mature and produce much fruit, thereby shaping their country and culture.

So, how can we—Christians who meet Chinese students while they're studying abroad—help them do that? By learning how to relate to Chinese students, share the gospel with them, and help them prepare to follow Christ in their own context, not just in ours.

---

6   One comment about the style—US English spelling, grammar, and punctuation conventions have been adopted for this book. I hope readers who use other forms of English will not find that distracting.

PART 1
The Need

1 What's Happening? A Picture to Aid Understanding

> *Ascribe to the Lord, all you families of nations,*
> *ascribe to the Lord glory and strength.*
> *Ascribe to the Lord the glory due his name;*
> *bring an offering and come before him.*
> *Worship the Lord in the splendor of his holiness.*
>
> 1 Chronicles
> 16:28,29

I would like to share a picture. It's a picture of a person's journey from China, to study abroad, and then back to China. It helps us understand a parallel journey: from life without Christ to life worshiping Christ. But first, here are some reminders of what the Bible says about this subject.

Jesus called people to "repent" (Matt 4:17)—that is, to have a complete change of attitude and behavior toward God. He said that to enter the kingdom of God we must be "born again . . . of the Spirit" (John 3:5–8). He declared himself to be "the way and the truth and the life" (John 14:6). He offered salvation: "I am the gate; whoever enters through me will be saved" (John 10:9). He urged people:

> "Love the Lord your God with all your heart and with all your soul and with all your mind." This is the first and greatest commandment. And the second is like it: "Love your neighbor as yourself." (Matt 22:37–39)

Time after time Jesus revealed what matters most: humbly acknowledging him (Matt 10:32) and being right with God, then following his loving, sacrificial example (Luke 10:25–37). These matter more than status (Matt 18:1–4; 23:8–12), ritual (Mark 7:1–8), wealth and financial security (Matt 6:19–24; 13:44–46; Mark 10:17–31). Jesus is even to come before family (Matt 10:34–37; Luke 18:28–30).

The Apostle Paul described the believer's new life, directed by the Holy Spirit, as demonstrating the "fruit" of "love, joy, peace, forbearance, kindness, goodness, faithfulness, gentleness and self-control" (Gal 5:22,23). Followers of Christ recognize a different authority (Col 1:16–18) and have different values (Rom 12:2), priorities (Matt 6:19–21), and purposes in life (John 15:16). Luke described the first believers forming a new community (Acts 2:42–47), and we see people groups being reconciled, as in the coming together of Jews and Gentiles to form the early church.

Hence, some students should be returning to China with radically changed ideas and priorities, revealed in various ways: in how they spend their time and who they spend it with; in changed relationships; in decisions about jobs; in how they use their abilities and money. The ideas behind the picture can help us understand what is going on when people leave their home culture, go to a completely different culture, profess faith in Christ, and then return to the original culture. They can also help us understand what *needs* to happen if returnees are to continue with Christ.

What Is Conversion?

Psychologist and theologian James Fowler interviewed hundreds of people about their lives and faith stories. He defined conversion as "a significant re-centering of one's previous conscious or unconscious images of value and power, and the conscious adoption of a new set of master stories in the commitment to reshape one's life in a new community of interpretation and action."[7]

I find it helpful to adapt this definition into a list of the *contents* of conversion:
- change in core values;

- change in ideas of where power and authority ultimately lie;

- a changed mental story of how the world works and one's place in it;

- commitment to a new community with shared beliefs and life—and, consequently, important new relationships.

Conversion involves a change in what and whom we put our trust. This reminds me of Paul's words urging the Christians in Rome not to conform to this world, but to be transformed by the renewing of their minds (Rom 12:2). With renewed minds they were to seek to live by God's values as his people—living out his story and purposes, under his authority, and through his power.

The Personal Framework or "What's in the Suitcase?"

Figure 2 illustrates the faith journey of a student leaving China, encountering Christianity abroad, and then returning home. More about the whole diagram shortly, but first let's consider a part of it: the suitcase. The suitcase represents what students bring with them from China and what they take back. For those who have come to faith abroad, the contents of the suitcase have changed because their *personal framework* has changed.[8]

---

7   James W. Fowler, *Stages of Faith: The Psychology of Human Development and the Quest for Meaning,* (New York: HarperOne, 1981), 281–82.
8   The idea of a "personal framework" comes from Charles Taylor's *Sources of the Self: The Making of the Modern Identity* (Cambridge: Cambridge University Press), 1989.

Personal Framework

Key

a = Values
b = Master Stories
c = Power Concept
d = Self Concept
e = Social Bonds

Figure 1: The Personal Framework

Everyone has a personal framework. It develops from birth, in relationship with other people, as we become aware of the world around us and start to respond to it. This framework informs our beliefs, feelings, and actions. Through it we interpret life's events, discern right from wrong, etc. The parts are listed next to the suitcase in Figure 1. You can see that they are pretty much the same things that James Fowler said change when someone becomes a believer.

Our *values* are those things which matter to us the most. Examples include being respected, being loved, glorifying God, attaining financial security, and experiencing justice.

Each person develops his or her own *master stories* or mental picture of how life works. These include worldview concepts, which are often shared by people in their culture: for example, "Is there a god/lots of gods/no gods?" "What happens after death?" They also include more personal ideas about what is normal, like "Women should be married by the time they are twenty-five." Living in communities of shared language and culture, we often develop shared stories.

As each of us grows up, we develop assumptions about who has *power* over us—such as parents, teachers, bosses, police, government, or God. Related to this is our *self-concept*: the ideas, both conscious and subconscious, of who we are and what our role in life is. This might include ideas like "I'm clever," "I'm not as pretty as my friends," "I need to come top in my class at school," or "I'm going to become a banker." Then there are *social bonds*: our relationships with the people and community who matter to us most and influence us most—e.g., family members, classmates, work colleagues.

If one part of the framework changes, the other parts are affected. Imagine that a person's master story changes to include a loving God who knows him and made him for a purpose. Well, then his self-concept changes: he starts to see himself as a loved child of God, rather than either as a hopeless case or a strong person in control of his own destiny. He sees that he has new brothers and sisters (the church) with whom he needs to spend time. Being with other Christians reinforces the biblical master story and helps him trust that ultimate authority lies in his Father God rather than in his parents or the government. Activities and aspirations that were important before are less important as values change.

People are often unaware that they have a framework until their values or stories are challenged. This can happen when there is a crisis and the old assumptions just don't work. It can also happen when they move away from their old relationships and community to a very different one—for example, as an international student.

Explaining the Picture

Now let's look at the larger picture with Figure 2. On the left, a Chinese student in China is about to set off with luggage, passport, and, of course, their personal framework. In the middle, they are abroad. On the right, they have returned to China with their Bible, new beliefs, and changed personal framework. The bar running across the bottom of the diagram represents the surrounding context that influences the student: the social contexts of China and their country of study, with their different histories and cultures. Church culture also varies from country to country.

Let's call our student Zhang. As he leaves China, Zhang is not consciously thinking about any of this! He does have values and assumptions about the way life works, however, even if he has never verbalized them.

What are his master stories? Might they include some worldview or big-picture stuff like: 'God? No, I don't believe any of that. I'm an educated guy, so I'm an atheist.' Grandma burns incense at the temple sometimes, and at festivals Zhang kowtows to the idols to please her. But gods and stuff—well, that's superstition. Zhang's life expectations? To get a good job, find a nice girl, travel the world. Relationships? Zhang struggles with his dad sometimes, and he wishes his parents would get off his back; but he'll look after them.

Anyway, let's get on that plane! A master's degree abroad—freedom!

Away from the demands of his home environment, Zhang has an opportunity to explore new places, lifestyles, and ideas. He meets people from different cultures and backgrounds, including Christians. He is puzzled. "Why do these people go to Globe Café[9] and talk to international students every week? Why are they so kind about offering rides? What do they want? Well, they don't seem to want anthing, but they sure ask some strange questions! Why do they do what they do?"

Then Zhang thinks, "They're harmless enough; I'll try this Bible study . . . Wow, these people are educated, and they actually believe God exists. Not only that, they think he is interested in them! What's going on? I like these people, I want to be with them, but I have never thought about these ideas."

---

9   Globe Cafés, popular in the UK, are organized by churches or Christian students to help international students feel at home, practice their English, and learn about Christianity—if they wish. These regular social gatherings go by various names, but Globe Café is the most common.

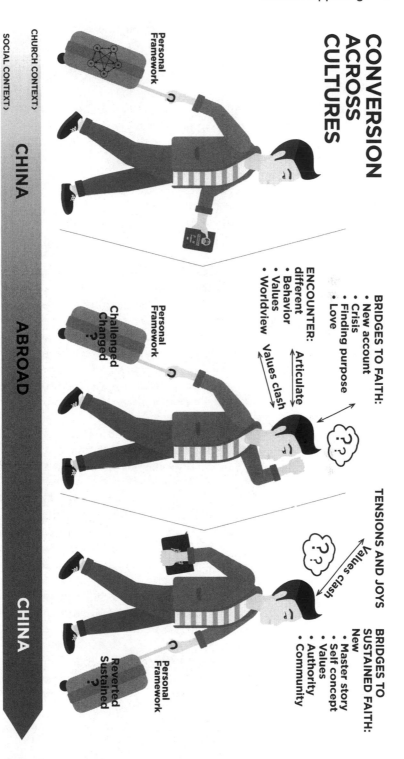

Figure 2: Conversion Across Cultures

As ideas and life experiences are shared, Zhang begins to analyze and test the Christian worldview. He starts to question his own beliefs.

Then he is invited to a party by a Malaysian Chinese classmate. There are lots of Malaysian and Singaporean Chinese there; but it turns out to be a Christian event, and all the Chinese are Christians. Zhang thinks, "That's not normal!" His ideas about religion, and even what it means to be Chinese, are challenged. He starts to realize he has certain assumptions about how life works. These Christians' beliefs clash with what Zhang has held to be true all his life. He starts thinking about who he is.

It's an emotional time for Zhang—both exciting and disturbing. It's exciting to hear stories of God acting in people's lives, and then to think about what God might do in his life. But it's also disturbing. Some of these new ideas undermine Zhang's long-held assumptions and values, particularly of those closest to him, like his parents and best friends back home.

An actual example may help here. A group of international students were discussing a case study about an East Asian Christian facing a choice between accepting a promotion at work or staying at the same level and salary (and possibly upsetting his boss). Taking the promotion would mean working on Sundays and not being able to go to church with his family. Several Christians said they would turn down the promotion, which some who weren't Christians thought was ridiculous. One person, though, who was shocked at the time later said that this was a milestone in her journey to faith. She suddenly realized the importance that Christians place on maintaining a close relationship with God and his people.

Back to Zhang, still studying abroad. He hears an account of the world, of history, and of himself that he has never heard before; and it seems more credible than what he has believed heretofore. This is his bridge to faith. Other people have different bridges, but this is his. He starts going to church, where he develops close friendships, including with Chinese Christians who speak his language. Zhang's new faith grows.

Then it's time to return to China (on the right in the diagram). People encounter different tensions and joys back home. Some experience more culture shock than others. Some experience more tensions because of their faith than others. Some settle into a church quickly; others don't. Zhang returns to China with a friend who also became a Christian abroad. They look for a church together, and meet to pray and read the Bible together.

Zhang views himself differently now: as a saved child of God with hope in eternal life. His biblical worldview strengthens his desire to honor his parents. Recognizing his own sinful yet forgiven state helps him forgive his father for beating him when he was a child.

However, Zhang values honoring his Father God even more. So when his father offers to use his connections to help Zhang get a safe government job with plenty of benefits, Zhang prays and then respectfully declines his father's offer. Zhang knows that in such a job he would eventually be required to make compromises with his faith, even to join the Communist Party. Honoring God has become one of his core values.

So what helps people like Zhang keep going in their faith? They have a clear idea of the biblical story and of themselves as part of it. They think of themselves as a loved child of a loving God who has ultimate authority. Because they esteem being with other believers, they seek out a church and develop bonds with people who share the same values and master story, people who encourage them to persevere.

Now let's consider another returnee, Fang. She too met kind Christians and attended church and Bible study regularly while abroad. She eagerly prayed a prayer of commitment and was later baptized. Fang told her friends how God answered her prayers, inviting them to go to church with her.

Unfortunately, a few months after returning to China Fang stopped going to church. This church was different than her church abroad, and she hadn't gotten to know anyone. And her life felt like a mess: Work was super busy, and her parents were pressuring her about marriage, but she didn't have a boyfriend. She wondered "Doesn't God love me anymore? Didn't I go to church enough?"

Fang's master story and values hadn't really changed. The kindness of people in the church abroad had touched her, but she hadn't understood the sacrificial love of Christ. Her notion of God remained as a fixer of problems in this life, and she lacked understanding of sin and eternal life. Or maybe she had a glimpse of these things, but they hadn't taken root.

Why Bother with Values?

Our values are powerful. They direct our feelings and behavior. They influence our relationships and the way we use our money, our time, our lives. Our values also matter to God.

In Athens, the Apostle Paul told his audience, "I walked around and looked carefully at your *objects of worship*" (Acts 17:23). There is a connection between worship and values. If we worship someone or something, we attribute worth to that object. Paul sought to understand the Athenians' objects of worship. I was doing something similar as I explored whether and how becoming a Christian had affected Chinese returnees' deepest values.

Values have various sources: some shared with other people, some relating to our unique life experiences. Ethnicity, nationality, class, age group (generation), education, and religion all affect values. Childhood and family are significant. Culture is a key source of values too.

Understanding our values and where they come from is important. For example, "Did I make that job decision because my ultimate value is financial security or because I believe God wants me to take on this role to serve him and grow to trust him more?" Or "Why do I constantly seek praise from people at work? Maybe this is getting in the way of my resting in God's love and salvation, and my revealing his love to others."

Sometimes we can help other people understand their values. When Xue was a new Christian in the UK, someone recognized her servant heart and gave her opportunities to serve. She was surprised by what God enabled her to do. Her trust in God grew, and she has gone on to serve in many other ways.

Yan had a difficult childhood, and consequently grew up valuing being in control. She experienced three crises, two abroad and one after her return. Then a pastor in China gently pointed out to her how much Yan valued being in control. Those crises and that insight helped her hand control to God and, in certain matters, to her husband. Their marriage, children, and ministries have all benefitted.

Paul tried to understand the Athenians' objects of worship before he shared the good news with them. He needed to do so in order to know how to share the good news with them. Their culture was so different than Paul's Jewish culture in Tarsus or Jerusalem.

The better we understand people's deep-seated values, the better we can convey the good news to them, choosing the most helpful Bible passages and relating our words to their situations. Additionally, the more we can help them understand their own values, the more we can help them bring their lives under God's authority. Jesus' challenge to the rich young man (Mark 10:17–27) is a wonderful illustration of insight into someone's deepest values.

Master Stories

Master stories comprise our worldview and our individual perspective on how life works. Darrow Miller defines a worldview as "a set of assumptions held consciously or unconsciously in faith about the basic make-up of the world and how the world works."[10]

A person's worldview consists of responses to fundamental questions like these: *Is there a God? What is real? What is a human being? What happens to a person at death? What is the meaning of human history?* An individual's worldview is usually shared by his or her community or cultural group.

William Wilberforce is a good example of someone whose changed worldview influenced his values and actions. His long battle against the slave trade came from a biblical conviction that all people have been created in the image of the God who created and cares about them. This is very different from, say, an animistic worldview that sees this world as illusory and people at the mercy of unpredictable spirits who need constant appeasing.

A person's master story also includes more individual ideas of how his or her future family life or career will map out in relation to others. For example, "In the UK, female university students normally live in shared houses with friends after they graduate."" Or "In Hong Kong, female university students return home and live with their parents until they marry."

Our master story includes our sense of what is going on around us. My father lived through World War II in Europe. His mental story of life was quite different than mine, since I was born long after the war. The story develops individually, as aspects of our community's worldview merge with our own life experiences.

---

10   Darrow L. Miller, *Discipling Nations: The Power of Truth to Transform Cultures* (Seattle: YWAM), 1998, 38.

Power and Authority

Faith in Christ involves a revised understanding of where power and authority lie, which in turn results in a transfer of loyalties. Gordon T. Smith identifies seven components of conversion in the New Testament: belief in Jesus Christ, repentance, trust in Christ Jesus, transfer of allegiance, baptism, reception of the gift of the Spirit, and incorporation into congregational life.[11] The distinction between believing in Christ and trusting in Christ is important. Believing Jesus said and did certain things is not the same as living dependently on him. That requires a transfer of allegiance to Christ, away from other allegiances that challenge his authority.

Self-concept

By *self-concept* I mean the ideas and identities people hold of themselves. For example, "I need to be strong"; "I am European"; "I get impatient easily"; "Nobody loves me"; "I am really good at tennis; etc. Our *self-concept* is intricately tied up with our master stories, values, and relationships with other people.

Social Bonds

When people follow Christ, the outcome is not just individual. Family members and others close to them are affected also. The believer becomes part of a different community, the body of Christ—a child of God with a new family of Christian brothers and sisters. As they identify with God's people and continue in congregational life, living out shared story and values, so the change deepens.

The new social bonds and transfer of allegiance to Christ can affect new Christians and their families differently; what is positive for believers may be perceived as a threat by their families. For example, while Christian Chinese returnee are enjoying a new sense of shared purpose and identity with their church "brothers and sisters," their blood families may experience rejection. This can seem worse if there parents view Christianity as a foreign religion, not part of their own master stories. They can feel betrayed or rejected—not just as family, but as Chinese.

The Significance of Context

The place and context we come from will contribute both to our conversion and to the impact of our conversion. This context is cultural, social, personal, and religious. The cultural part is the intellectual, moral, and spiritual atmosphere and the myths and rituals that underlie it. The social part includes tradition, living conditions, important relationships, and institutions. Our personal histories add to the mix, as do our prior religious ideas and experiences and

---

11   Gordon T. Smith, *Beginning Well: Christian Conversion and Authentic Transformation* (Downers Grove, IL: InterVarsity), 2001,125.

those of the people around us. The political and economic situation can also affect people's faith journeys.[12]

The modern history of China contributed to large numbers of well-educated mainland Chinese turning to Christ while in the US in the 1990s. The suffering and failed experimentation of Mao's rule and the later Tiananmen Square Incident in 1989 led to disillusionment, trauma, and a loss of identity. Many then were searching for alternate sources of meaning; widespread social, personal, economic, and political upheaval contributed to an openness to new answers, a new narrative, and ultimately to God.[13] Today's China is rather different. Yet the stories in this book show that the contexts from which Chinese students come still influence their responses to Christians and the Christian message.

However, the context abroad also affects how Chinese students respond to Christians and Christ. The location of churches and the activities of Christians play a big part in attracting Chinese students to attend churches and investigate the Christian faith.

Chinese students visiting Chinese churches in the US have been shocked by the generosity and kindness of church members. These people didn't just behave like traditional Chinese in caring for family members; they looked after the students—complete strangers—and clearly expected nothing in return.[14] It makes a difference when churches provide social activities and Bible studies for international students. It makes a difference when local Christians invite students into their homes. It makes a difference when Christian Chinese students befriend newcomers on campus.

Bridges to Conversion

The friendliness and activities of Christians were what initially made students in my research curious about Christianity. But what helped them actually *believe?* They described four common bridges to faith. Some experienced more than one.

First bridge: A new account of life

Some were like Zhang: they heard a new account of life and found it credible. At first they went to Bible study groups out of cultural curiosity, to relieve their boredom or loneliness, or to practice English. Some met Christian Chinese students; others met locals. They became interested in the content of the Bible studies and in the lives and motivations of the Christians. Eventually they decided that they believed what they heard.

Changlan provides an example of this bridge. From primary school onward he loved exploring new ideas. As an undergraduate in China, his appetite for reading grew into an interest in the world beyond China, encouraged by watching

---

12   Lewis R. Rambo, *Understanding Religious Conversion* (New Haven, CT: Yale University Press), 1993, 22.

13   Fenggang Yang, *Chinese Christians in America: Conversion, Assimilation, and Adhesive Identities* (University Park, PA: Pennsylvania State University Press), 1999, 84–93.

14   For one example see Andrew Abel, "Favor Fishing and Punch-Bowl Christians: Ritual and Conversion in a Chinese Protestant Church," *Sociology of Religion* 67, no. 2 (2006): 161–78.

foreign films and meeting international students in his city. Meeting Christians abroad was a way to continue exploring new ideas.

Second bridge: Crisis

While she was in the UK, Luli's boyfriend in China broke up with her. She then had no money to complete her studies, because he was her sponsor. She also heard that her dear brother had terminal cancer. In the midst of crisis, Luli believed God was calling her to him, giving her a second chance.

Two other people used a Chinese Christian saying when reflecting on their crises: "The end of a human being is the beginning of God." Previously they had depended on themselves; now things seemed so out of control that they felt helpless. But with this came a new openness to God.

Third bridge: Searching for purpose

Before leaving China, Xue already believed somewhat in a single God. She wrote in her diary that while she was abroad she would seek the purpose of her life.

Baozhai had met foreign Christians at a university in China at a time when her faith in communism was collapsing. She arrived in the UK looking for something to fill the gap.

Fourth bridge: Love

Xiaodan found love within the Christian "family." She had been seeking security and love since childhood, when she lived in fear of her father. She had been driven by achieving academic success as a desperate bid to be valued. She embraced the Christian teaching about God's love being demonstrated through Christ, because she both heard it and experienced it as "real life, real love, real family." A local couple welcomed her and a Malaysian "brother" into their family. Their character and behavior were consistent with the message their community was declaring.

And God at work

Central to these stories is an active God. Those I interviewed talked about God acting in their lives, turning them to him. They didn't simply make independent decisions to believe something and then change their lifestyle accordingly. One referred to a "sunset" in her head when she first believed. That reminded me of what Luke said about Lydia. As she listened to the Apostle Paul, "The Lord opened her heart to respond to Paul's message" (Acts 16:14).

Encounters and Challenges After Return

Those who turn to Christ while they are abroad find that their whole framework starts to change. As their worldview moves into line with the biblical worldview, they see themselves differently too. They strive to thank and honor God, and not to hurt him who died for them. They want to tell their families. Values change. Strong bonds form with other Christians.

But when they return to China, the context changes again. Family members, with the associated joys, tensions, and responsibilities, are much closer. The foreign university environment is exchanged for the Chinese workplace. Church is different. Again, the framework and master stories are challenged.

Different cultures endorse different values. The classic statement from the Westminster Shorter Catechism that "Man's chief end is to glorify God, and to enjoy him forever" is very different than the atheistic outlook of most mainland Chinese. Also, Chinese culture places great importance on harmonious relationships; to honor others you must know your place, keep the peace, and not disturb the norm. So if your churchgoing offends or upsets important people in the hierarchy, like parents or the boss, what do you do? How can you keep going despite the concern and shame it causes people you care for deeply?

While they are abroad, some Chinese students may behave like a Christian, going to church and even being baptized, without actually believing that Christ died for them. People from group-oriented cultures sometimes do things abroad because those things seem proper there, or as a way to show respect and gratitude to their host Christian friends. Change in behavior does not necessarily mean that underlying values have changed. If they haven't changed, the student will probably give up that behavior after returning home.

Returnees face various challenges: relating to parents, the jealousy or suspicion of coworkers, even feelings of no longer belonging. Some feel they have let their family down because they haven't achieved the higher paid job and status their families had anticipated. Some experience an intense feeling of loss, almost like mourning.

Returnees to China also face government restrictions on access to international social-networking websites, which can constrain relationships developed abroad. However, Skype, FaceTime, and Weixin, or WeChat, the Chinese networking app, offer great opportunities for contact with friends worldwide, even if they are accessible to government monitors.

All returnees face a variety of challenges and opportunities. The new believers among them face additional ones. Some immediately find a church they like, share their faith with family and friends, and find jobs that allow them enough time to connect with God every day and serve him. But they are in the minority.

Others stop attending church after one or two visits—quickly succumbing to work, family, and societal pressures.

Others struggle but persevere, settle in church, and gradually make Christian friends who become a source of mutual encouragement and challenge them to grow in faith in Christ—and eventually they go on to produce a crop.

How Can We Help?

In addition to all the ways we would help a seeker or new believer from our own country, we need to do extra things to help people from cultures different than our own. If we are really going to help our friends returning to China, we need to acknowledge those cultural differences, learn about China and Chinese students' values, and adapt our evangelizing and discipling. It's doable. Our Chinese friends can help us. I think the rest of this book can too!

PART 2
The Context

2 Change, Culture, and Education

When Mrs. Zhou went to visit her hometown, her old friends came to see her. Their sons and daughters drove them—in expensive cars that they had bought their parents. She returned to Beijing thinking, "Yes, my son has a PhD from overseas and has been back a while now. It's only proper that he should buy me a Mercedes-Benz."

Expensive consumer goods are very visible in China now. Parents who have invested heavily in their child's education may have expectations of a certain lifestyle. Children who provide these goods, this lifestyle, show their parents due honor. They are *good* children.

The combination of superfast change and high expectations of education mixes with certain traditional values. This synthesis shapes the students we meet. It also provides returning new Christians with some interesting challenges and opportunities.

China Today: Opportunity and Change

On my first visit to Beijing, in 1996, people were flying kites everywhere. I even saw children flying kites in the median strips between divided highways (British readers know them as the central reservations on dual carriageways). A few years later the kites and kids were gone, replaced by lanes of car after car. By 2001 I was staring in amazement at the smart apartment blocks in Shenzhen and admiring the facilities at the new school where my returnee friend taught. I remember arriving at Shanghai Pudong Airport in 2004 and feeling like a country bumpkin. Sleek limousines pulled up to collect the designer-suited Chinese businesspeople standing near me. Traveling on the subways in Beijing, Shanghai, and Guangzhou a few years later, I appreciated all the information in English. In Changsha, capital of Hunan Province, Mao's heartland, I was bewildered by the selection of colorful shoes in the department store—more choices than I had at home!

The rise of millions of Chinese people from poverty to prosperity in thirty years is astounding. The literacy rate increased from 66 percent to 97 percent between 1982 and 2016,[15] and average GDP per capita increased from $309

---

15 UNESCO Institute for Statistics, World Bank's website, http://data.worldbank.org/indicator/.

in 1980 to $8583 in 2017.[16] However, the increase in prosperity varies from province to province.[17]

China has the world's largest number of internet users. In 2017 there were 1.17 billion mobile internet users in China, most of them accessing it via their phones.[18] Some Chinese students recently told me that the WeChat app (Weixin) is the greatest development in China. They can order taxis, pay for meals and shopping, find their friends, talk to their parents, share music, and a host of other things I would never imagine. In 2017 the Chinese internet company, Alibaba, overtook Amazon, to become the world's largest e-commerce company.[19] In 2017 Beijing's Tsinghua University was ranked the world's top university for engineering, ahead of the National University of Singapore and the Massachusetts Institute of Technology.[20] China is changing fast.

Constraints and concerns

Yet constraints exist. The government bars access to Google, Facebook, and a variety of other websites. So although returnees can visit some Christian websites, they may not be able, for example, to download sermons from their church overseas. Traffic on the web and social media is monitored and censored, as is television. Some hotels provide television access to the BBC and CNN, but what is shown is still censored.

One day I was watching CNN in my room in a Beijing hotel, part of a well-known international chain. Suddenly the TV screen went blank for a couple of minutes. The date was June 4. CNN had broadcast a piece about the anniversary of the 1989 Tiananmen Square Incident; the Chinese censors simply stopped the broadcast during that piece. Yet Chinese Christians use WeChat and other social media to great effect for both connecting and advertising.

Pollution is a huge concern. I know people who have moved thousands of miles from Beijing and other cities, though still remaining within China, to escape pollution. An enormous scandal occurred between 2008 and 2010 when powdered milk was tainted with melamine. The safety of food products still worries Chinese citizens.

The 2008 Sichuan earthquake revealed both positive and negative aspects of today's China. The government's rapid response was impressive, and the access afforded the media was unprecedented. Individual Chinese also responded generously: some sending money, others going themselves to care for victims. But after the earthquake accusations were made that poor standards in the construction of school buildings in the 1990s had contributed to the devastation.

16   https://knoema.com/atlas/China/GDP-per-capita
17   For example, in 2017 the GDP per capita in Beijing was equivalent to US $20356 , while in the western province of Gansu it was US $4647. Even in Hebei, the province nearest Beijing, it was only US $7606. https://www.forbes.com/sites/salvatorebabones/2018/02/12/china-quietly-releases-2017-provincial-gdp-figures/#50be361a20dc
18   China Internet Watch website, https://www.chinainternetwatch.com/21925/mobile-data-h1–2017/.
19   https://www.bloomberg.com/news/articles/2017–10–10/alibaba-tops-amazon-to-become-biggest-e-commerce-company-chart.
20   "Best Global Universities for Engineering," *U.S. News and World Report*, http://www.usnews.com/education/best-global-universities/engineering.

Some claimed that public money meant for building schools had been siphoned off.[21] Indeed, the fight against corruption is a central plank in the program of President Xi Jinping. Investigators attributed the 2015 Tianjin chemical explosion that killed 165 people and injured hundreds to widespread mismanagement and lack of regulatory oversight.[22]

Such disasters affect returnees directly. One returnee I know took time to go to Sichuan to help earthquake survivors. Another, away at the time of the Tianjin explosion, works in that area.

Experience is mixed. Despite these concerns, many people, including most returnees, enjoy a standard of living and degree of choice way beyond anything experienced by previous generations. Others, unable to keep up with the intense consumerism and competition, lose out. They suffer the consequences of a cutthroat working environment unrestrained by mature regulatory institutions.

The speed of change

A television documentary told the story of a teenage girl who left her rural home to work in a distant city during the building of the Three Gorges Dam. When she returned three years later, her home had disappeared. The hills and countryside had been swallowed up in the sprawl of the massive urban area of Chongqing, which has a population of over thirty million. In the time it takes to travel abroad to study for a degree, landscape, lifestyle—everything familiar—can all disappear.

The speed of change has shortened the length of a generation. Different generations experience different events and have different memories. Sometimes it's hard for children and parents to understand each other because they have experienced and seen such different things.

I was chatting with Fei, a twenty-four-year-old student from a big entrepreneurial city in East China. Fei spent her spare time window-shopping. She had just been to the London sales and bought her mother a dress. But Fei was upset. She thought the dress would really suit her mother, but her mother was annoyed with her! "How much did the dress cost?" I asked.

She replied, "£300"—which was a lot of money to me. I thought about it. Fei's parents were probably born in the 50s or early 60s and lived through hard times, when people struggled to get by. When Fei was born, China was ten years into its period of opening up to the world. By the time she started school, East China was already very different from the decades of hardship.

I asked, "Did your parents build up the family business from nothing?" "Yes," she said. Mother and daughter had such different life experiences and attitudes toward money.

Differences in life experience can also affect returnees' efforts to share their faith with parents. Saying grace before a meal led to a sharp rebuke for one returnee:

---

21   "Sichuan Earthquake Killed More Than 5,000 Pupils, Says China," *The Guardian*, May 7, 2009, https://www.theguardian.com/world/2009/may/07/china-quake-pupils-death-toll.

22   Javier C. Hernandez, "Tianjin Explosions Were Result of Mismanagement, China Finds," *New York Times,* February 5, 2016, http://www.nytimes.com/2016/02/06/world/asia/tianjin-explosions-were-result-of-mismanagement-china-finds.html?_r=0.

"*We* provided your food, not this god of yours!" The parents heard the prayer as a dismissal of all their years of hard work providing the child's expensive education.

Other parents just want their children to stop talking about their "foreign ideas" and behaving differently than others. They have lived through times when attracting attention, instead of conforming, brought painful consequences.

The degree of change in China can bewilder us, as foreigners looking on, too. China is huge, and situations vary. What happens in one place may not be the same as what happens in another, or in the same place at another time. The church's situation is a case in point. A phrase often used by writers about China is "In China, everything is true somewhere, sometime."

Values in flux

The speed of change, combined with China's size, means there are many influences on values. One psychologist referred to an increase in the "divided self" in a "divided state."[23] The breakdown of Maoist communism and the development of the market have generated competition between value systems. The huge rise in living standards has been a great blessing. Yet some see the massive growth in consumerism as a sign of increasing, ruthless individualism. To combat this, some advocate a return to traditional Confucian values, emphasizing care for parents and loyalty to country.

Government interest in values can be seen in the slogans chosen by each of the last three presidents: "Build a well-off society" (Jiang Zemin); "Build a harmonious society" (Hu Jintao); and now, Xi Jinping's "Chinese Dream." Values are taught throughout the education system, from primary school to university.

Chinese Values

The immense population includes people from diverse backgrounds. The cosmopolitan cities of the east contrast with the vast rural areas of the west. Coastal Fujian has developed traditions different from the cities on the old Silk Road to Central Asia. People of different ages and ethnic groups have been exposed to various ideologies: Confucianism, Buddhism, Daoism (also known as Taoism), communism, consumption-driven market economics, Western movies, even Islam.

The extent to which the values and issues described below apply to any individual Chinese will vary, but evidence suggests that they apply to many Chinese students overseas. This list is not exhaustive. It just indicates areas where Chinese peoples' values may differ from those of non-Chinese. Some of these values may sit happily alongside new Christian values; others may not. Some may be strengthened in a context of Christian belief, while others are weakened.

China's Confucian heritage remains deeply influential. China is still representative of a group-oriented society that emphasizes face, social harmony, and

---

23   Arthur Kleinman, et al., *Deep China: The Moral Life of the Person: What Anthropology and Psychiatry Tell Us about China Today* (Berkeley: University of California Press, 2011), 288.

family. These characteristics are intertwined and particularly influential in the child-parent relationship.

Filial piety (Being a good child)

Confucian philosophy emphasizes obedience to authority and right behavior in a hierarchy of relationships, especially within the family. Scholars refer to this as "filial piety" (*xiào* 孝). At its core is the relationship between child and parent: the dutiful child shows parents gratitude and respect, cares for them in old age, and generally behaves in a way that brings honor to the family. Filial piety also affects other intergenerational relationships within the family, along with relationships outside the family. Chinese children, of course, often feel great love and appreciation for their parents, as well as show it.

For various reasons, providing for their parents' old age is a big issue for many Chinese students. The financial burden on a single child needing to provide for two parents and four grandparents is one reason. Legal requirements may be another. Recently some areas have introduced laws allowing parents to demand payment from their children if they are unable to provide for themselves.[24] Concern about *face* is another reason.

Face and proper behavior

Face relates to reputation. Concern for one's own face and the face of others can be supremely important. Face is "the respectability and/or deference which a person can claim for himself from others, by virtue of the relative position he occupies in his social network and the degree to which he is judged to have functioned adequately in that position as well as acceptably in his general conduct."[25] Chinese people recognize an interconnectedness with others that Westerners generally don't have or don't feel. More than simply an individual feeling of deep shame or embarrassment, loss of face affects a Chinese person's web of relationships and the individuals in those relationships.

For example, even when parents and grandparents can afford to provide for themselves financially, their offspring aren't necessarily off the hook. Some families would suffer great loss of face if the children aren't seen to provide generously. This can pose a dilemma for Christian adult children. The Bible teaches both good stewardship of money *and* honoring parents. So what do they do about their underpaid church pastor, or that work with migrant kids God has placed on their heart? Remember Mrs. Zhou and her friends' expensive cars? That's an example of how regard for such status symbols can become intertwined with notions of proper care and respect for parents.

There is another side to this, though. Caring for the family extends beyond the parent-child relationship. Chinese can be very generous in supporting a sibling's or cousin's education, which is much more generous and sacrificial than many of us foreigners.

---

24 For example, in 2013 the government of Qufu, Confucius' hometown, stipulated that all citizens should pay their parents a monthly allowance and take them for a monthly haircut and an annual physical. Xiaoying Qi, "Filial Obligation in Contemporary China: Evolution of the Culture-System," *Journal for the Theory of Social Behaviour* 45, no. 1 (2015): 141–61.

25 David Yau-fai Ho, "On the Concept of Face," *American Journal of Sociology* 81, no. 4 (1976): 867–84.

Marriage in China is not just about two individuals, but two families. Some parents simply want their daughter to be provided for well or for their son to be cared for by a decent woman. Other parents can be very demanding. A mixture of motives related to finances and face can contribute to parents' absolute refusal to accept a certain boyfriend or girlfriend as a potential marriage partner for their child. This situation is even more painful for the Christian who wants to marry only another Christian.

Widespread use of the term "left-over" to refer to unmarried women over the age of twenty-seven increases pressure on single women and their parents. Men have their own pressures: the marriage market demands they have a car, an apartment, and savings. Without them they are considered a *san wu nan* (三 无 男), a "three-withouts man."[26]

Even if parents are not at all demanding, the child may still be deeply concerned about face. As a teenager, Xifeng failed in her first attempt at the university entrance exam. So her parents had to ask relatives and friends for the money necessary for Xifeng to change to a different subject and take the exam again the next year. She felt she had shamed her parents terribly, shamed herself, and failed in her duty to be a good child. Later, contrasting her life as a Christian with her earlier life, Xifeng said:

> Before, I wanted to find a good job and earn lots of money to make my parents proud, because they did a lot for me. They gave me everything they have. Yeah, so it's my responsibility to glorify them . . . You know, to make them look good in front of other people.

When Fuyin failed to get a job abroad after completing her master's degree, she didn't want to go home because this failure would cause her and her parents to lose face.

Newly returned Ling found a church that, in order to keep their meetings quiet, moved from place to place. She knew they were good people, but the secrecy made her feel they were behaving shamefully—"like thieves." Added to that, it felt wrong not to spend Sundays with her parents. So Ling stopped going to church. Culturally, the right thing to do in this dilemma was to fit in with social norms and obligations, to 'honor the hierarchy first, your vision of truth second."[27]

Putting family first is very important in China. This affects decision-making, including how money and time are spent. What for some nationalities would be purely individual decisions, such as whether and when to get baptized, are for Chinese matters that have much wider repercussions; parents and others must be seriously considered.

Some other cultures tend to be much more lax and less aware of other people. We need to remember that the Chinese combination of doing the proper

---

26   For more on this and the lives of Chinese twenty-somethings, see Alec Ash's *Wish Lanterns: Young Lives in New China* (London: Picador, 2016).

27   Michael Harris Bond, *Beyond the Chinese Face: Insights from Psychology* (New York: Oxford University Press, 1991), 151.

thing and according people the respect their age or position merits can affect our own relationships with Chinese students.

Ping had been reading the Bible with a British Christian. Ping did not yet believe, but when the lady asked her if she believed she said "yes" because, to her, that was the kind and proper thing to do; to say no would have damaged both individuals' face and represented very improper behavior toward such a kind lady, who was also older than Ping. Misinterpreting Ping's politeness as agreement, the British woman asked Ping if she wanted to repeat a prayer of commitment. Ping, of course, felt obliged to say "yes." Eventually Ping did come to faith in Christ, but the process required the involvement of other Christians, including Chinese, who were able to assess Ping's real position.

This example shows how easy it is to make mistakes about what Chinese students believe. I've had many conversations with Christians in China who have tried to help returnees referred to them by Christians overseas. The referring people describe the returnee as a new Christian, but often that person is not a believer at all. He or she enjoyed the friendship abroad, but sees little relevance in continued contact with Christians once back in the home environment.

Face and reciprocity

Ping's case highlights the importance placed on reciprocity in relationships. The belief is that parents have sacrificed so much for their child that the child can never do too much to pay them back. But that's *inside* the family. *Outside* the family is different. One should never become too indebted to someone; a balance needs to be kept. If a person keeps giving, the recipient may start to wonder "What do they want?" or "When are they going to call in the return favor?"

This can play out in different ways in our relationships with Chinese students. They might feel more comfortable to accept help if they can give something in return—like contributing food for a meal rather than being fed all the time. On the other hand, when Chinese students experience the kindness of Christians who are strangers but expect nothing in return, this can be a great witness.

Relationships, harmony, and group identity

Are you a straw in a bundle of straws or a ripple in a pond? That's how Fei Xiaotong, the father of Chinese sociology, pictured the difference between Western and Chinese social relationships.

A Westerner is a separate individual with membership in several different groups—for example, work colleagues, a sports team, immediate family. This person is like a straw in a bundle. The straws may touch and affect each other, but a single straw remains the same when it is taken out of the bundle. And the other straws retain their individual identities when one straw is taken away.

The Chinese person, however, is at the center of a widening circle of relationships, like the ripples made by a stone thrown into a pond.[28] Ripples merge into each other. As they touch other ripples they change, and the other ripples change too; then that affects others. And since Chinese relationships are hierarchical, some ripples make

---

28   Xiangqun Chang, on Fei's book *From the Soil: The Foundations of Chinese Society*, first published in 1947, http://personal.lse.ac.uk/changx/Book_English.htm.

big waves. The parent-child relationship and the boss-employee relationship are two with huge potential for wave-making!

Westerners are more like self-contained units that retain their individual identity in different contexts. For the Chinese, people and things are always part of their environment and therefore change as that environment or context changes.[29] This goes a long way back. The Western emphasis on personal freedom goes back to Greek philosophy. The Chinese emphasis on harmony goes back to Confucius. In Confucian ethics, worth and self are found in harmonious relationship with others rather than in individual identity or truth. So in China what is deemed proper behavior can vary from situation to situation. It depends on the relationships and people involved. It depends on your *guānxì* (关系), your network of relationships.

Chinese students may change their behavior while abroad but not continue after returning to China. Church attendance is an example. If returnees haven't had a change of master story, if they don't see themselves as the child of a loving Father God and a member of his worldwide family, they will give up attending church. It feels too disruptive to family or work relationships. Or it just feels weird to be with people they don't know. Going to church starts to feel like a foreign activity, something they did in Toronto or Atlanta but not something suitable for Nanjing.

It can be hard for us, as non-Chinese, to see what is going on. We don't see the situational constraints on a person's behavior, whereas East Asians do.[30] We need to work with Chinese Christians who know the mainland context so that we can help new Chinese believers identify the relational constraints that might pull them away from church and following Jesus back home.

Chinese can be very loyal to people in their in-group—their family, closest friends, even work colleagues—but not feel obligated to people outside that group. Therefore, getting involved in charitable or volunteer work may seem odd. A British friend who helped start an orphanage in China was repeatedly asked why by puzzled locals. This in mind, imagine what a difficult concept tithing must be for new Christians, let alone for their families.

The desire for quality: Suzhi

Harvard Girl Liu Yiting: A True Chronicle of Suzhi Cultivation was published in 2000. Liu's parents groomed their daughter for Harvard from the age of two. The book is a manual of how to build your child's *suzhi*.[31] *Suzhi* (素质) is hard to translate. The word *quality* comes closest, as in the phrase "a person of high quality." It was China's best-selling book for sixteen months.[32] Responses to the book varied: some copied its child-rearing methods; others criticized its materialistic values.

---

29   Richard E. Nisbett, *The Geography of Thought: How Asians and Westerners Think Differently . . . and Why (London: Nicholas Brealey Publishing, 2005).*

30   Ibid. See Chapter 5.

31   Andrew Kipnis, "Suzhi: A Keyword Approach," *The China Quarterly* 186 (June 2006): 295–313.

32   John Schauble, "US School Story a Huge Chinese Hit," May 6, 2002, *The Age*, http://www.theage.com.au/articles/2002/05/05/1019441458295.html.

The authorities share this desire to increase people's quality. The English lessons that they provided for taxi drivers in the run-up to the Beijing Olympics provide one example. A friend who recently returned from China mentioned another; he appreciated that people at railway stations were now forming queues instead of all rushing for the gate together.

So *suzhi* is not necessarily problematic; it depends how the term is understood. It can mean different things to different people. One person might use it in the sense of high moral standards. Another might connect cosmopolitanism and academic achievement with *suzhi*, and perhaps also connect those things with affluence and a consuming lifestyle. This can lead to a dangerous linking of different qualities, all of which are considered *suzhi*. For example, the logic could go like this: "*Suzhi* means being morally virtuous. Having a high-paying white-collar job and being able to afford a nice apartment is also to have *suzhi*. Therefore, to have a nicer apartment than someone else is to be of higher quality." So someone who chooses a simpler lifestyle may be viewed as of lower quality or moral character.

Christian returnee Qingzhao took a job with lower pay to avoid working on Sundays. She and her husband couldn't afford the larger car and apartment her mother thought fitting for Qingzhao's status as an educated returnee. Qingzhao was criticized harshly by her mother, who thought that if her daughter had a large flat and expensive car that would show the whole family's *suzhi* (or quality). Qingzhao, meanwhile, wanted to honor God (to increase God's face) and strengthen her faith by going to church. She didn't think they needed a bigger apartment or car, or that having one would increase her quality.

Honor and shame

Several authors have described the world's cultures in three main categories: honor-shame, innocence-guilt, and power-fear.[33] Beliefs and practices vary among the many cultures and countries with an honor-shame orientation—for example, between the Middle East, Japan, and China. As I mentioned earlier, China's culture is group-oriented rather than individualistic and therefore highly values face (or honor), relationship, and hierarchy.

Jackson Wu comments that when people in an honor-shame culture give face, they show that they love or respect the other person; and having face gives people a sense of security. And he adds, "People in honor-shame cultures tend to see their identity in terms of their relationships."[34] Respect for those higher in the hierarchy (parents, ancestors, community leaders) is important.

This matters in our relationships with Chinese students. For example, those of us from more individualistic cultures tend to make our decisions, including the decision to follow Christ, in isolation. Decisions made by Chinese students, on the other hand, will affect a range of other people. If they don't pray and think through those effects in advance, they may hurt others and struggle after their return.

---

33   Roland Muller, Jackson Wu, and Jayson Georges are three.

34   Jackson Wu, "Does the 'Plan of Salvation' Make Disciples? Why Honor and Shame Are Essential for Christian Ministry," http://www.patheos.com/blogs/jacksonwu/2016/02/04/does-the-plan-of-salvation-make-disciples/. Jackson Wu is a leading voice in the "honor-shame" discussion; more of his ideas can be found on his blog via the link above.

The Bible attributes great importance to the church (the group) and the individual believer's place in it. Many new Christians surely fall away when they return because they have only understood, or been taught, their new faith as an individual relationship with God; they are unaware of being born again into the family of believers. They will particularly need that new family once they return to China, where they will typically be drawn back into old groups and away from Christian influence.

The case has been argued recently that much of the Bible was written in and about "honor-shame" or more group-oriented cultures but is often communicated purely in the language of more individualistic, law-based Western cultures. Jackson Wu and Jayson Georges write that many Bible stories, verses, and situations that speak to an honor-shame mindset are overlooked, thus limiting the full and fruitful communication of the gospel.[35] This doesn't mean there is a different gospel for different cultures. Rather, we need to recognize that the gospel is multidimensional so that we can mine and share it more deeply.

Education

Education is a national value in China. There is a huge amount riding—for the whole family—on success at school and university. Children, parents, and grandparents may all depend on the child's future income. Some people have adequate savings, but others are dependent on the only-child generation.

Competition starts early. Preparing children well means they may get into a good primary school. Those who do best in primary school have access to higher ranked middle schools. To get into a good high school you must do well in a good middle school. Which high school you go to determines what kind of college or university you can try for. Then the two-day national university entrance examination, the *gāokǎo* (高考), determines exactly what level of institution you will attend, if any.[36]

The high school years leading up to the *gāokǎo* are intensely stressful. After a long ten-hour school day, students spend more hours studying in order to keep up with others. If you fail to secure a high enough exam mark and rank for your desired institution and course, you won't be able to go there.

Study abroad

Study abroad is expensive. For example, for the 2017–2018 academic year, the UK University of Birmingham's international student fee for one year of an undergraduate engineering degree was £20,250,[37] more than $28,000. This doesn't include living costs, which could easily exceed £10,000 ($14,000) a year. A one-year master's student could need £30,000 ($42,000) and someone doing

35   Jayson Georges, *The 3D Gospel: Ministry in Guilt, Shame, and Fear Cultures* (Time Press, 2014). For Wu, see above.

36   For more on the gaokao, see Alec Ash, "Is China's Gaokao the World's Toughest School Exam?" *The Guardian*, October 12, 2016, https://www.theguardian.com/world/2016/oct/12/gaokao-china-toughest-school-exam-in-world.

37   https://www.birmingham.ac.uk/undergraduate/fees/fees.aspx.

a three-year undergraduate course upwards of £90,000 ($125,000). In light of this, Chinese students' reputation for hard work makes great sense. That their families are willing to fund such costs reveals the perceived value of a foreign education. Parents are investing for their own future as well as their children's.

Other parents have different motives. Huifang spent a year as a visiting professor in the UK. She appreciated the slower pace of life there. Four years after returning to China, she took her son to Canada to complete his secondary education because she wanted to remove him from an education system she considered too burdensome for children. Another attraction is that competition for entry to some foreign universities is not as great as for entry to some Chinese universities.

Summary: Change *and* Tradition

China is changing. Today's students travelling abroad are different than those born ten years earlier. Academic visitors (staff of Chinese universities who spend time at our universities) are different than students. However, while certain traditional Chinese values are being challenged, they still exert strong influence. We need to look out for the effects of face filial piety, and group identity without making too many quick assumptions.

Those studying abroad are often highly driven. Their parents, and the students themselves, have high expectations upon their return. Societal expectations urge returnees to compete, own more, and acquire status. All of this can distract returnees from the time and focus needed to find and settle in a church and to express and share their faith.

Yet technology, increased economic and social freedom, and even social problems themselves afford opportunities for new ways of working, socializing, and for serving others outside the family. Those committed to following Christ are finding opportunities to honor him and make him known.

3 The Effects of Context—History, Politics, and Work

If you asked Chinese undergraduates about the Opium Wars or the "unequal" treaties, they might be a bit embarrassed, but they would probably know what you were talking about. They would have learned in school that British opium traders brought social devastation to China and that foreign governments then took control of several major Chinese ports.

However, the students probably wouldn't think these nineteenth-century events affect them now. But they do. They contribute to their government's concerns about foreign interference. These political consequences affect returnees in regard to church, of course, but also at work.

The Modern Chinese Historical Context

Recent history will have influenced students' family backgrounds, though it's important to remember that people are not affected in the same way or degree. The Cultural Revolution impacted the childhoods of several, but not all, of the returnees whose stories are told in this book. Comments here are brief and limited to the period since the foundation of the People's Republic of China (PRC). It's worth knowing more, so please refer to the reading list at the end of the book.

1950s: Early years of the People's Republic

The PRC was founded on October 1, 1949. Known in China as the "liberation," this date is celebrated annually with a week-long national holiday. The early years of the PRC and the rule of Mao's Chinese Communist Party (CCP) were a time of relative order and relief after a long period of civil wars and brutal invasion by the Japanese.

Things started to change in the 1950s, however. Land reform programs increased, redistributing land from landlords to peasants. Peasants were encouraged to overthrow landlords, many of whom were killed. Then, in the 1956 Hundred Flowers Campaign, Mao invited intellectuals outside the Party to share ideas, even to criticize the Party. . The extent of the criticism this unleashed led to a terrible backlash, the Anti-Rightist Movement. A million intellectuals were affected; many lost their jobs or were sent to labor camps in the distant countryside.[38] Some families were separated for years.

---

38   Richard Curt Kraus, *The Cultural Revolution: A Very Short Introduction* (New York: Oxford University Press, 2012), 7.

The Great Leap Forward, in 1958, was intended to harness the labor power of China's huge population to bring about economic growth. Though it did produce a few positive outcomes, such as roads and infrastructure, it was otherwise catastrophic. Campaigns like those to get the whole population to make steel in their backyards and the Kill a Sparrow Campaign (消灭麻雀运动; *Xiāomiè Máquè Yùndòng*) brought economic and environmental devastation. It all contributed to the Great Famine of 1959 to 1961, which led to the deaths of about twenty million people.[39]

So even before the Cultural Revolution there was widespread poverty and suffering. The institution of the family, so important to the Chinese, was also undermined: many families were split up and people were formed into large production communes.

The cultural revolution

Mao initiated the "Great Proletarian Cultural Revolution" (1966 to 1976) to purge China of capitalism and "bourgeois" traditions and instill Maoist thought. People deemed to be reintroducing old ways were termed "revisionists" and were to be removed. This was a time of turmoil and violence.

Mao encouraged schoolchildren and older students to form Red Guard brigades. They were to lead the removal of the "four olds": old customs, old culture, old habits, and old ideas. Disorder was allowed, the idea being that the masses rather than the ruling class should lead the revolution. This and the vagueness of the definition of the four olds led to terrible atrocities. Red Guards destroyed the property of people they arbitrarily decided were "bourgeois." Schoolteachers and university lecturers were persecuted by students, some even killed. People were forced into intensely shaming public self-criticism. Many individuals committed suicide. Some children even betrayed their own parents for having an "old" book, such as a Bible, or an "old" object, such as a violin. Trust was destroyed between neighbors and in other social relationships—even within many families. A legacy of pain and mistrust leaves its marks to this day.

Education was devastated in the Cultural Revolution. Universities closed for over four years. The fathers of three of my research participants had no education beyond primary level because all schools and universities closed from 1966 to 1968.[40] Another said her father was branded a landowner and, despite being an educated man, was reallocated permanently to a menial construction job.

For many the material and emotional effects lasted long after the end of this terrible period. Changlan's father values education extremely highly because his own education ceased in 1966, at age eleven. His career never advanced beyond working in restaurant kitchens. The effect this had on his relationship with his son is described later in Changlan's story.

---

39   Jonathan Spence and Annping Chin, *The Chinese Century: A Photographic History* (London: HarperCollins, 1996), 181.

40   James C. F. Wang, *Contemporary Chinese Politics: An Introduction* (Prentice-Hall, Englewood Cliffs, 1989), 276.

Although students we meet today were born long after the Cultural Revolution, their parents may well have lived through it. Parents' early experience of sudden changes in government policy can understandably make them concerned about their children doing something out of the norm that could draw official attention. They also greatly value today's good standard of living. For some, their experiences affected their marriages and parenting.

Continuing implications of history

Although the Cultural Revolution ended in the 70s, hardship continued well into the 80s. Material and political necessity separated many families. Yan's parents had no choice but to leave her with her grandmother for five years, when she was two, while they traveled many miles away to work. Yan recalled,

> Before seven years old, I don't know what my parents look like. I was born in '76, and then China is very poor. So they can't visit us regularly, maybe twice or once a year.

When Yan, at seven, moved to live with her parents, she felt like a stranger in the house, especially because her younger sister had lived with their parents from birth. After completing her degree, Yan embarked on a fiercely competitive legal career to gain more money, status, and influence. In our conversations, she referred to herself repeatedly as having been a "controller." She linked her former intense drive to achieve with the insecurity arising from being taken from her grandmother at the age of seven to live with parents she barely knew.

Even many of today's undergraduates have spent several years away from their parents. In 2015 I met a twenty-three-year-old who didn't live with her parents until she was fifteen. Her parents weren't poor, but because they were so busy working she lived with her grandparents. When she finally moved into her parents' apartment, she spent her time either at school or in her bedroom studying. Then she went to university and later abroad. Now about to return to China to live with her parents again, she was scared; she had no idea how to function as an adult in her parents' company.

Of course, family relationships vary in China, as elsewhere. Some students have closer relationships with their grandparents than their parents, or struggle to relate to parents with life experiences so different than their own. Others have very warm relationships with their parents. Whatever their family background, Christian returnees often have a real burden to share the love of Christ with their parents. Some Chinese-speaking overseas missions even provide activities to help Chinese students do so when parents visit their children studying overseas.

Because of wounds caused by parental abuse or neglect, some struggle to forgive their parents. God does bring healing, enabling them to forgive and reach out to their parents, but it isn't easy. Fuyin said:

> Ever since I believed in God, I forgive my parents. We were beaten when we were young, so I still had great hatred inside me. But like the [letter of Paul to the] Romans said, when you believe in God, the love from heaven pours on us.

Research in the US in the 1990s identified the experience of turmoil, through the Cultural Revolution to the 1989 Tiananmen Incident, as a major factor in the conversion to Christianity of that generation of mainland Chinese abroad.[41] A later study pointed out that younger students' lives were "less disturbed than those of the earlier immigrants," but that they experienced other dramatic changes related to the Deng-era reforms.[42]

I believe some born after the worst turmoil still suffer from it because it affected their parents and the way their parents treated them. Psychologists refer to this as *transgenerational trauma" because it has passed from survivors to a second or third generation.* For example, Fuyin (born in 1973 to a comparatively elderly father) attributed her father's violent temper to his army experiences, fighting both the Japanese invaders and in the civil war.

Seven returnees in my research spoke of having deep peace because God was now in control of their lives, even in the face of difficulties. Four of those were women with an unhappy childhood. The distress that three experienced, and the extended separation from parents of another, were probably caused by events of that time which affected their parents. The suffering their parents had experienced, or the shame caused by their inability to provide for their family, may have led to the fathers' anger or absenteeism.

Nevertheless, it should not be assumed that everybody had a tough childhood. Others described happy childhood memories in loving families.

Deng and the Reform Era

With Deng Xiaoping in power, the 1980s saw the opening up of China to the economic ideas of the outside world and to trade and cultural exchange. Massive strides were made in the material situation of the Chinese people. However, the decade ended with the brutal oppression of the Tiananmen Incident of May and June 1989.

For weeks people around the world watched television coverage of students, later joined by workers, filling Tiananmen Square and creating the Goddess of Democracy statue. Students in other cities also held demonstrations. One academic told me that he, a student himself at the time, took a train from Anhui Province, hundreds of miles away, to join the students in Beijing. There was idealism, excitement, and hope. This turned to despair as the army opened fire.

Different accounts have been given of what happened, and not all of the footage available outside of China is accessible in China. Today's younger generation may know little about these events,[43] but some of their parents know.

---

41   Fenggang Yang, *Chinese Christians in America: Conversion, Assimilation, and Adhesive Identities* (University Park, PA: Pennsylvania State University Press, 1999), 84—93.

42   Yuting Wang, "Religious Conversion to Christianity Among Students from the People's Republic of China: A Comparative Study" (paper presented at the Annual Meeting of the Association for the Sociology of Religion, San Francisco, CA, August 14, 2004), http://hirr. hartsem.edu/sociology/wang.html.

43   While researching her book, *The People's Republic of Amnesia: Tiananmen Revisited* (Oxford: Oxford University Press, 2014), Louisa Lim showed Beijing university students the famous photograph of "tank man" facing a line of approaching tanks. Only fifteen out of one hundred knew what it was.

We can understand why they would encourage their children to enjoy what they already have, get on with earning a living and looking after the family, and avoid activities and philosophies that might cause unwanted attention.

These parents are also grateful that recent governments have maintained stability. After Deng's death in 1997 his successors led China into the World Trade Organization in 2001, helping the nation to overtake Japan as the world's second-largest economy in 2010. The Chinese people have seen great increases in their living standards, opportunities to enjoy life, and personal freedoms.

Pursuing the China dream

Since becoming president in 2012, Xi Jinping has extolled the "China Dream." Some interpret it as China becoming the world's greatest power. Some dream of studying hard to help their country. Schools and universities have provided walls for students to write their dreams on.[44]

For many, the dream is materialistic. With the collapse of communism, globalization is arguably the major contributor to China's changing values, particularly through access to foreign media and the internet. This encourages consumerism. Shopping, certainly window-shopping, seems to be almost a national pastime. My Chinese language textbook even mentions it in the lesson on hobbies.

Some people simply appreciate having access to a wide range of goods and the money to buy and enjoy them with family. Others have an intense desire to acquire more money so that they can possess more than others. The artist Li Kunwu spelled this out trenchantly in his autobiography.[45] Written in graphic-novel form, *A Chinese Life* has three sections: "The Father" (i.e., Mao); "The Party" (i.e., the CCP); and "The Money." Kunwu depicts money as the ruler and main object of worship in China today.

Some returnees find this competitive acquisitiveness extremely stressful, since the pressure to conform is high. Some, however, are relieved; now, as Christians, they don't feel the need to have the same status symbols as friends, such as a bigger car or apartment. They have courage to turn down jobs that interfere with family or church life, because having lots of money is now less important to them. Their self-worth and security are not tied to their material possessions.

Even some who are not Christians say the Chinese would do well to relax and enjoy life more instead of spending all their energy pursuing material wealth.

---

44   http://www.bbc.co.uk/news/world-asia-china-22726375.
45   Li Kunwu and Philippe Otie, *A Chinese Life* (London: SelfMadeHero, 2012).

The Political Context

The complexities of contemporary Chinese politics are beyond the scope of this book. I will just mention a few examples of effects on returnees.

Party membership

In 2015 the CCP had eighty-eight million members,[46] about 6 percent of the 1.4 billion population. Although Communist Party members are still required to receive political instruction and uphold the socialist way of life, many are more attracted by the status membership implies and the benefits it affords than by Communist ideals. Party membership and certain senior jobs go hand in hand—for example, in government, police, and universities.

Party members are forbidden religious affiliation. Some Christian returnees have resigned Party membership, while others have not. One twenty-four-year-old, chosen for the Communist Youth League (CYL) as a teenager, decided to ignore phone invitations to meetings until they stopped. She was junior enough for that to happen. When I asked if she could resign from the Party, she said that would look like she was dishonoring her country, would be a disgraceful blot on her record, and would affect many things, including job applications and buying property.[47]

I have encountered increasing concern among academics returning as believers. One was very worried, because while he was abroad his Party secretary told him he would have to leave the Party (and his job) if he acquired a religion. Since his return, in 2017, the Party secretary has made several unannounced visits to him at work and talked a lot—but not mentioned faith. The returnee has been quietly keeping his head down, but does attend a registered church each week.

Older CCP returnees may be fearful of losing their pension if they make their faith known.

Some returnees, like Changlan, are not members and avoid jobs that could lead to expectations to join. This can cause conflict with family members who can't understand this apparently foolish or ungrateful rejection of benefits and security. Grandparents can't understand why their children would allow *their* children to miss out on educational opportunities available only to Party members' children.

On the other hand, at least one urban house church welcomes CCP members in the congregation , though without allowing them a leadership role.[48]

---

46   http://news.xinhuanet.com/english/2015–10/22/c_134737141.htm.

47   A Chinese friend who has lived abroad for seven years was told by her Beijing-based parents that the party recently phoned them to ask about her. She became a member as a young person, but after becoming a Christian stopped paying her dues and responding to correspondence. That was seven years ago, but they still had her records.

48   Gerda Wielander, *Christian Values in Communist China* (New York: Routledge, 2013), 11.

Politics at school and work

Even outside the Party, atheism is still the norm—although interest has increased in both Buddhism and Christianity. Religion is dismissed as superstition; and science and technology, along with Chinese socialism, are deemed the only way forward. School education has changed greatly since the 80s, but the political and the moral are still combined in the classroom. Chinese university students are still taught Mao Zedong thought.

Some jobs are affected by politics more than others—particularly in state-run organizations, academia, and the law. Min, a returnee teaching in a university, was quiet about her Christian faith but did not hide it. She was picked out for monitoring by her department's Communist Party officer. This woman submitted a highly critical report to the university authorities. But then they conducted their own review of Min's work, found it to be excellent, and commended her!

In contrast, when another young academic who was living in campus accommodations was reported to the authorities by a neighbor for holding Bible studies in her flat, she was demoted.

It is particularly difficult for returnees who are Party members. As Christians they may wish to leave. Even if they are prepared to face consequences themselves—such as difficulty finding a suitable job—they may be unwilling to cause their family shame and difficulties. One recent returnee knew that if she tried to leave the Party, or disown her membership, her parents could lose their jobs too. Also, the Party may simply not allow her to leave.

Christian lawyers are of interest to the authorities, particularly because Christians have been prominent in taking on human rights cases. One returnee described how her lawyer husband had been "invited for a cup of tea" by officers of the Public Security Bureau. Although he wasn't involved in politically sensitive cases, he had studied abroad. The officers made it clear that they knew a lot about him. They asked him to join a certain association of Christian lawyers and then report to them about the people in the group. He refused and went back to work.

Civil society

The authorities' concerns aren't limited to religious activity. They are wary of groups, religious or not, that bring large numbers of people together outside of government oversight—for example, professional groups, such as lawyers, and churches that grow too big.

Since 1979, civil society and the charitable sector have grown. Even some unregistered churches have established charitable projects. These may remain small because they lack legal status, thereby lacking the means to publicize or show financial accountability. Yet churches are finding ways to serve their local communities—for example, providing food banks or tutoring for children of migrant workers—and to do this with the informal support of local officials.[49]

---

49   Brent Fulton, *China's Urban Christians: A Light That Cannot Be Hidden* (Eugene, OR: Pickwick, 2015), 77.

Some house churches have started schools with a Christian curriculum, but this is difficult. Other Christians have started private schools legally, following the state curriculum, but employ Christian staff and promote a Christian worldview through the way lessons and relationships are conducted. I know returnees who started such a school; some parents were impressed enough to explore Christianity and attend church.

It remains to be seen whether this can continue. Religion particularly has been coming under government radar in the past few years.

Foreign NGOs have established medical, developmental, and educational projects. Even NGOs with known Christian affiliations have been welcomed, provided they agree not to use this as a platform for evangelistic activities.

In 2016 new regulations were introduced to govern foreign NGOs operating in China. This may be an indicator of Xi Jinping's administration's concern to contain the influence of foreign ideas and the growth of civil society. President Xi has made it clear that foreign influence in religious matters is particularly unwelcome.[50] Also, in September 2017 new religious regulations were announced.[51] Their implications will only be fully understood after they come into force in 2018 and beyond.

One-child policy

The one-child policy was introduced in 1979. It was later relaxed somewhat, with certain couples allowed a second child (when their first child was physically disabled, both parents were only-children themselves, or both were from ethnic minorities). Since 2016 all couples have been permitted to have two children. Penalties for breaking the rule vary, including heavy fines, forced abortion, and loss of employment. Those having children illegally would not be able to get them their all-important *hukou (户口)*, or local identity card, which is needed to enroll for school and other essentials.

The implications of this policy have been huge. Family expectations and financial pressures on only-children were discussed in chapter 2. Another effect is the perception of abortion among young Chinese. When I asked a UK university medical doctor about the pressures of his work, he told me he was greatly disturbed by the high number of Chinese students asking for abortions. Many consider abortion a form of contraception.

Shortly after arriving abroad to work on their master's degrees, Yan and her husband discovered she was pregnant, which caused her to delay her studies for a year. In the meantime she met Christians who supported her when she was feeling isolated, shocked, and struggling with English. Both Yan and her husband became believers. And after the baby was born, both of them eventually completed their degrees.

Yan accepted a position in a prestigious law firm back home. Just before returning home she discovered she was pregnant again. Her battling emotions

---

50   https://www.theguardian.com/world/2015/may/21/president-xi-jinping-warns-against- for-
    eign -influence-on-religions-in-china.
51   https://www.chinasource.org/resource-library/blog-entries/new-religion-regulations-to-take
    -effect-in-february.

and her decision to honor God are described later in this book. When she became pregnant a *third time*, in China she left China temporarily, to give birth abroad in order to ensure that her daughter had identity papers. Yan, her husband, and the grandparents all faced criticism (and some envy) because Yan did not have an abortion.

Most Chinese students abroad are only-children. Although there are benefits in being the sole focus of parents' and grandparents' attention, some struggle to relate to and share with others because they have not had the experience of growing up with a sibling.

Work

Working life is tough. Lvery ong hours are commonplace. One returnee described how, to show commitment, he always had to get to work before his boss arrived and leave after his boss left. The expectation to work on Sundays is common; and sadly, many give up on church. Some people have a Monday to Friday working week but many work six days.

I have, however, heard of returnees praying before job interviews, then mentioning their desire to attend church on Sundays and being granted their request. One English teacher was permitted time off for church on the condition that she found a replacement to teach her classes; every Sunday she did.

Two returnees eventually gave up their seven-day-week banking jobs without sight of another job. Some find ways of having church fellowship midweek. Others deliberately choose jobs with lower pay and fewer promotion prospects, but fewer hours, so that they have time for family, church, and rest. Some parents support this approach; others see it is as unfilial.

Some female returnees have given up working while their children are young; they want to look after their children in a way that their own mothers could not. Also, they hope to share Bible stories and Christian values with their children, which a non-Christian nanny or grandparent would not. Some can afford giving up paid employment; others sacrifice comforts that their peers can afford. Some treasure the time with their children, but miss the intellectual stimulation that comes with working.

Bosses can exert great power. Male returnees describe being required to take part in work banquets and heavy drinking with customers. One returnee had to drink so much that he needed surgery; his doctor told him he would die if he didn't stop. His boss, who had already had alcohol-related surgery himself, ordered him to keep drinking.

Sometimes the evening ends with the expectation of joining the boss and important customers in being "treated" to the attentions of prostitutes. Getting out of such situations, while also retaining the boss's face, is very hard indeed.

One returnee, a senior teacher, wanted to return abroad to do a PhD, but his boss refused, saying he wouldn't even allow him to apply for another job until the boss himself retired. The boss had the power to do that.

Another returnee was frustrated by the expectation that employees buy gifts for their boss. I have often heard the phrase "complicated relationships" in relation to certain unwritten rules in the work environment having to do with hierarchy, gift-giving, and meeting others' expectations.

Starting his own business, another returnee was worried how he would reconcile his Christian principles with the widespread custom of paying bribes and "treating" officials and clients in order to win contracts.

Enci refused to follow the normal practice of telling customers whatever they wanted to hear, even if it wasn't true—for example, telling them it would be possible to deliver their order on a certain date when she knew that wasn't the case. At first Enci was criticized by colleagues, but gradually they accepted her "odd" behavior as part of her faith.

Some returning new Christians look for work in large multinational companies, which generally have less challenging practices.

Sticking to biblical principles can be costly. A company that supplied drugs to hospitals came close to bankruptcy when the Christian owner refused to go against biblical teaching. He would not pay bribes, join tax-avoidance schemes, or break his promises. Staff left and other business leaders shunned him. He had to change his business to another sector. Now his profits are a fraction of what they were, but he has no regrets.[52] Also, the prayerful, long-term obedience to God of business leaders like him has impressed others. Weary or shameful of the old ways, they investigate the source of Christians' strength and trust Christ themselves.

In 2015 the Shandong Dongying Christian Businessmen's Fellowship was started.[53] A Christian website reported that churches in several cities were creating fellowships to encourage Christian businesspeople to reform business culture.[54] Such fellowships provide mutual support and a chance to identify biblical business methods. Although they cannot form an official national network, they surely network informally through social media.

Certain job types seem to constrain open Christian faith more than others. Of the nineteen participants in my PhD research, six held university or government-related posts; and of these six, only two attended church regularly. These two were in relatively junior positions, one—who was married to a Christian—having deliberately chosen not to pursue promotion in order to maintain a strong family and church life. The three oldest female academics, two professors and one senior lecturer, and a man with a central government job, were not attending church. That said, there are senior academics who lead house churches.

The type of work unit can affect returnees' willingness to be open about their faith. State-run organizations are monitored more closely by the Communist Party. In recent years, central government has issued directives to university teachers about limiting the influence of foreign ideas in their classrooms.

---

52   Liang Chen, "Between God and Mammon," *Global Times*, February 27, 2014, http://www.globaltimes.cn/content/845019.shtml.

53   "Shandong Founds Christian Businessmen's Fellowship, Aiming at Social Service and Philanthropy," October 2015, translated article posted on ChinaSource's website, http://www.chinasource.org.

54   http://chinachristiandaily.com/2016–03–31/ministry/zhongshan-ccc-tspm-organizes-business-as-mission-fellowship—guangdong_871.html.

School and university teachers are monitored, presumably because they have such influence over China's youth. Some Christian academics, however, have managed to build an informal network.[55]

These days there are more opportunities for original work contributions, including Christian service. For example, Xing became a self-employed lawyer and Luli worked in a small HR consultancy, options which might not have been open to them in the past. Others have followed online management or leadership courses based on Christian principles.

Some returnees are very proactive. Yin runs a workplace Bible study group. She prayed and found a Christian colleague; they started meeting and then others joined them, including some who were not Christians.

Yin and other returnees have shared how God has helped them to be gracious when colleagues mock their faith or get angry about their refusal to be involved in dishonest practices. Although the Chinese workplace is tough, there are many opportunities to share Christ and a great need for biblical values.

55   Paul Golf, *The Coming Chinese Church: How Rising Faith in China Is Spilling Over Its Boundaries* (Oxford: Monarch), 2013, 96.

4

The Effects of Context—Religion

China is an atheist country. Song's mother consulted a shaman about her daughter's education. Two married physics PhD students used astrology to choose their baby's name. If church growth continues at the recent rate, by 2030 China will have more Christians than any other country.[56]

Aren't these contradictions? What's going on?

Buddhism, Daoism, traditional Chinese folk religion, and atheism are all influences. Christianity is starting to have an impact too. Maoism may have collapsed in disillusionment, but the Communist Party is still treated semireligiously by some. Science and scientific materialism (i.e., believing only what is seen or what scientists say) are taught throughout China's education system.

School students are taught that there are five official religions: Buddhism, Daoism, Islam, Catholicism, and Protestant Christianity. These five are formally acknowledged and allowed to apply to register places of worship. Other practices may be labeled "superstitions" or, in some cases (such as Falun Gong), "evil cults."

Many Chinese students consider themselves to have no religion, but when asked if any of their relatives ever go to the temple, they might say, "Oh that—superstition—yes." Older relatives may pray and sacrifice to various gods in regard to their grandchildren's exam results, or consult shamans about career decisions or marriage partners. Some students may have even been dedicated as children to, for example, the Buddhist goddess Guanyin. Fortune-telling and consulting horoscopes are common.

Buddhism, Daoism, and Syncretism

Interest in Buddhism is increasing in China. However, if a student says they are a Buddhist it is best not to assume they adheres to a specific branch of Buddhism, as described in a textbook, but to find out what they personally believe and practice. They may well mean a mixture of Buddhism, Daoism, and folk beliefs and traditions. This Buddhism could be quite different from the Buddhism in, for example, Sri Lanka or Thailand.

This syncretism (adding to one religion practices or beliefs from other religions) goes back at least two thousand years to when Buddhism was introduced from India. Making sacrifices, practicing divination, and employing shamans go back over three thousand years—well before the time of Li, who is believed to have founded Daoism and to have lived about the same time

---

56   http://www.kukmindaily.co.kr/article/view.asp?page=&gCode=7111&arcid=0010724477
     &code = 71111101.

as Confucius (sixth century BC). The mother who consulted a shaman and the physics students who used astrology, mentioned above, would be hard-pressed to attribute their practices to a particular religion. People who identify as Buddhists and people who identify as Daoists might take part in the same festivals (along with people who claim adherence to neither religion)—although they have different reasons for doing so.

Students exploring Christianity abroad can adopt this "pick and mix" approach too. Their thinking might go something like this: "If my uncle's business got that big contract after my aunt bought incense at the temple and that Christian woman's illness was healed after her church prayed for her, why don't I try both to pass my exams? Why not get both Chinese *and* Western gods on my side?"

Pragmatism

Underlying such syncretism is a deep cultural pragmatism. Cambridge anthropologist Adam Yuet Chau has argued that the main driver of Chinese religion is *efficacy*, the capacity to achieve a required result.[57] Someone with a problem might try going to a Daoist temple, a Buddhist temple, then a church or mosque, *and* consulting a spirit medium if each seems not to work.

Chinese students visiting churches abroad are probably thinking, "Does it work?" They want to see if this "God"—or perhaps this process—will give them their desired exam results, career, or marriage.

Festivals and Spirits

Regard for family reputation and proper family relationships continues beyond the grave in China. For many, this merely represents respect or love for the deceased. For others, behavior at funerals and festivals includes worshiping ancestors. Despite Confucian and atheistic influences, many people still believe in spirits.

Festivals during which returnees may be expected to worship their ancestors include Qingming (or Tomb-sweeping Festival) and the Lunar New Year. At Qingming, some families simply visit and tidy up their ancestors' graves, while others pray to their ancestors or bring food and burn paper money so that the ancestor doesn't lack anything. Some travel long distances to visit graves; others just enjoy a family get-together.

Death rituals and funerals are particularly challenging for Christians. The oldest son is expected to take a leading role. Dealing with these matters is hard, especially when the entire family is upset by the loss of a loved one. We can help returnees by encouraging them to pray and work out an appropriate biblical response to these expectations in advance. They need to know what the rituals

---

57   Adam Yuet Chau, "Modalities of Doing Religion and Ritual Polytropy: Evaluating the Religious Market Model from the Perspective of Chinese Religious History," *Religion* 41, no. 4 (2011): 547–68.

actually mean to their family members so that they can act in a way that honors God, yet still show respect and care for family.[58]

Following the first two of the Ten Commandments can lead Christian returnees into family conflict at Chinese festivals, marriages, and funerals in which ancestors are worshiped and other rituals—originally intended to scare off evil spirits—are practiced. Even in cases where relatives don't believe in such spirits, not taking part may seem extremely disrespectful and uncaring. The situation is worse when a relative believes the deceased will be caused great anguish if not worshiped and may even bring bad fortune on the family.

There are other potential difficulties for returnees whose family members have been involved in other religions or the occult. First, there are potential misunderstandings about God and the Christian faith. Some Chinese may see "the Christian God" as another god who needs to be appeased or sacrificed to so that the worshiper can receive blessings of wealth, health, and success. This is very different than seeing God as the Creator who is holy and loving and wants people to know him.

Second, there is a possibility of demonic attack, a subject that many churches avoid. I have heard Chinese people refer to bad things happening after another member of the family became a Christian. One friend had nightmares months after her mother's death; she was convinced that her dead mother was suffering, and angry with her, because she had not worshiped her mother properly at the funeral. Some people are tormented by anxiety, strange experiences, or nightmares as new Christians; they may have been dedicated to a god as a child or might be depending on some "protective" amulet given to them by a relative.

Satan may use such ruses, and family involvement in the worship of idols and ancestors, to attack East Asian Christians—especially new believers. It is important to help them get rid of any items and practices that keep them trusting in other gods. They need to confess to God, renounce the problem practices, ask for God's forgiveness, and seek his help to overcome any temptation to revert to old ways.

Chinese seekers and new believers need to be taught the reality of spiritual warfare, as in Ephesians 6, and the importance of trust in Christ alone. We need to help our friends think biblically and pray about how they will behave in relationships with relatives—continuing to honor their parents and elders, but honoring and trusting Christ more.[59]

---

58   Adam Chau's article includes a short section on five different concerns that inform Chinese funeral practices, providing insight into traditional attitudes to death and the afterlife. See http://www.ames.cam.ac.uk/faculty/publications/chau/chau-modalities-of-doing-religion-and-ritual.pdf/view.

59   Such ministry needs to be appropriate, sensitive, and timely. Talking about demons with new Christians who haven't been adequately taught might scare them away from Christianity or lead them to excessive interest in the demonic.

Modalities of Religion

Chau points out a fundamental difference between attitudes toward religion in China and in areas like Europe that have a long history of Christianity. In short, he argues that the most important thing for mainland Chinese is not the big idea of the religion—or, in the case of Christianity, God himself—but the ways of doing it: the processes of religion. Chau has identified five *modalities*, or ways of doing religion, in China: the discursive-scriptural, the personal-cultivational, the liturgical, the immediate-practical, and the relational. I can see these ways at work in the lives of students and returnees I have met.

Neither Xing nor Jiang was attending church when I met these two men separately, in Beijing. However, each described how much he valued small group meetings abroad, where beliefs were discussed and the Bible was applied to personal and theoretical situations. Jiang said he never really enjoyed going to church abroad, but his wife loved it. He has a social science PhD and Xing is a lawyer; maybe they are both more comfortable with discussion (the discursive) than with singing and one-way preaching in church (the liturgical) or other church group activities (the relational). Perhaps discussion itself was what mattered to them, rather than being part of the people, or church family, that God is building.

People with different personalities and backgrounds naturally prefer different ways of worship, but if the process (e.g., self-improvement or rituals) is more important than the reason for the process (e.g., reconciliation with the God who made us) in a person's view, then that person may not be trusting Christ for salvation. At the heart of new life in Christ is a change of worldview and a transfer of allegiance to a new authority.

It is also worth noting that China does not have a centuries-long history of congregational worship. Chinese religious activities have traditionally been individual, such as going to the temple, or in a family group, such as funerals. The returnees I know who have continued in their faith and in church have a revised worldview—with a new Father and a new family of Christian brothers and sisters. The significance of these social bonds is the subject of chapter 9.

Confucianism

According to Chau, educated elites in China have traditionally tended toward a mixture of the discursive and personal-cultivational modalities. Their desire to improve themselves fits with Confucian values.

I have seen this in PhD students and visiting scholars. One Chinese professor saw the Bible as a source of good philosophy and Jesus as a sage, or model of a good man. Confucian philosophy teaches that man is inherently good and perfectible; here was a book to help him with that. When asked what it would mean for him to become a Christian *as a CCP member*, however, he was perplexed as to why there would be a contradiction. His idea of being a sinner was that he needed improvement; he didn't have a sense of owing allegiance to the God who created and loved him.

Although Confucianism is not widely perceived as a religion, it influences Chinese ideas of religion.[60] In addition to emphasizing self-improvement, it stresses the ideal of a compassionate and benevolent ruler and the correct performance of rituals. Chinese scholars abroad can interpret biblical teaching, Jesus, and church activities in a similar light, thereby missing the deity and uniqueness of Christ and the grace of God.

Confucian thought is secular; it lacks a cosmic, supernatural perspective. The Bible describes where people and the cosmos have come from and where they are going, and it points people to future personal redemption. Confucius did not do this. Rather, "His philosophy sought the redemption of the state through righteous individual behavior. Oriented toward this world, his thinking affirmed a code of social conduct, not a roadmap to the afterlife."[61]

This stems from a worldview that is very different than that of the Bible and helps to explain why so many Chinese are pragmatically seeking an effective way of living rather than a big picture that explains history.

Islam

Some Chinese students, typically from the Hui or Uyghur ethnic minorities, are Muslim. Hui come from a variety of places in China, but Uyghurs tend to come from the northwest. Although most Hui female students abroad don't wear a headscarf or show outward signs of being Muslim, they may have deep family connections with Islam.

One returnee who took part in church and Bible studies abroad didn't come to faith in Christ, but some years after returning to China she started attending a Bible study. Her parents' imam traveled all the way from Henan to Shanghai to try to stop her. More encouragingly, another Hui returnee to Shanghai was so changed by her faith in Christ that her mother started attending church too.

The Chinese authorities have national security concerns regarding serious unrest and violence in border provinces, such as Xinjiang, that contain large populations of ethnic minorities.[62] This is a result of events both outside and within China, including terrorist attacks carried out in other provinces.[63]

Christians in China, particularly in Xinjiang, need to act with great care when discussing faith with Uyghurs and others from Muslim backgrounds. Evangelism of Muslims is prohibited. Tensions and restrictions even constrain Uyghur Christians' participation in registered churches.

---

60 The veneration held for Confucius can border on religion. At a celebration for Confucius' descendants in his hometown of Qufu in 2009, people bowed before an altar to Confucius, where a sheep, bullock, and pig had been sacrificed (Peter Foster, "Confucius Family Tree Unveiled," *The Telegraph*, September 25, 2009).

61 Henry Kissinger, *On China* (New York: Penguin, 2011), 15.

62 Xinjiang's neighbors include Kazakhstan, Kyrgyzstan, Tajikistan, and Afghanistan; Uyghurs have cultural affinities with Central Asia.

63 For example, attacks by Uyghur separatists in Kunming (2014) and Guangzhou (2014 and 2015) and a car explosion in Beijing (2013)—in addition to bombings in Xinjiang. Criticism has also been leveled at the authorities for encouraging large-scale Han migration to Xinjiang.

The Christian Church in China

Excellent books and websites about the history of the church in China, its amazing growth, and its relationship with the government are available. Some are listed at the end of this book. The following section is selective, focusing on the church as it is experienced by returnees.

At the end of the twentieth century the Chinese church had a reputation for being largely rural, female, elderly, and less educated. This situation has changed, particularly in provincial capitals and the large cities of East China. Beijing, Shanghai, and Chengdu, for example, contain churches with large numbers of students, young professionals, and returnees. Though these churches are comprised of both men and women, women still tend outnumber men. And some provincial capitals, unfortunately, still lack such churches.

Li, a new believer returning to Hainan in 2016, did find a good church, though it was different than what she expected. The Bible teaching was solid, and a young teacher in the church befriended her; but she was the only returnee. The congregation of about forty met in an apartment, and the pastorhad a busy full-time job in addition to family responsibilities and preaching four times a week. The nurturing she experienced abroad was unavailable; she had to be self-disciplined to have quiet times and to initiate finding ways to serve.

Types of church

Churches are required to be registered with the State Administration for Religious Affairs (SARA). Registered Protestant churches are part of the Three-Self Patriotic Movement (TSPM) and sometimes known as "three-self churches." Some churches prefer not to be registered with the government for theological reasons and to avoid potential compromising of church integrity. Others have applied for registration but been refused.

Although people often categorize Chinese churches as two types, "registered" and "unregistered" (or, somewhat unhelpfully, "official" and "underground"), the reality is more complex. Unregistered churches are often known as "house churches" or "family churches." House churches may indeed meet in a house or apartment, but they may be considerably bigger and meet in rented facilities—for example, a hotel conference room. Some unregistered churches operate clandestinely; others keep a low profile and are left alone, although the authorities know about them. Freedoms and restrictions vary from place to place and time to time.[64]

The large cities that returnees typically move to will have different kinds of house churches.[65] Some may be part of traditional urban house church networks, while others are made up of migrant workers from rural areas and have connections with established rural church networks. A third kind is the urban house church that has started independently, usually in this century, and consists mainly of young professionals, including returnees. They often decide

---

64   New religious regulations, introduced in February 2018, will further affect such freedoms and restrictions. Exactly how awaits to be seen.

65   For deeper insight into the church in China, see Brent Fulton's *China's Urban Christians*.

to be open about their activities, but vary in how they do that. Some keep a low profile and intentionally remain small (say, under fifty members), while others have been more direct with the authorities.[66]

Returnees attend both registered and unregistered churches, although most I know are involved in unregistered churches. Some find larger registered churches too impersonal for close fellowship.

Three returnees I know initially attended two churches simultaneously: a registered church with an English-language outreach, opportunities to serve, and a young-marrieds group, as well as a large house church led by a famous pastor committed to unrestrained preaching of the Bible. All three have since settled into just one church—two in the registered church and the other in a smaller unregistered church.

The church in China today

Church numbers and freedom have both grown hugely over the past thirty years. The relationship between church and state has changed too. As the church has grown to where it probably has as many members as the CCP, the government seems to have accepted its presence somewhat. Here's how religious sociologist Fenggang Yang summarizes the government's view of religion:

> Since the 1990s, the Communist Party-State has affirmed that religion could have both positive and negative social functions. It may contribute to society through charity services as well as teachings that provide spiritual solace and moral guidance to ordinary people. Nonetheless, religion is the opium of the people that may lead people to anti-social beliefs and may be used by adversary forces for political causes.[67]

The government undoubtedly wants to control this growing social force; but ome registered church welfare initiatives, such as poverty relief, marriage counseling, and elderly care, have been encouraged. Although this affords opportunities to share the love of Christ, this doesn't mean that churches can do whatever they like. Where they are seen to threaten stability, or certain vested interests, action is taken. The government motto remains "Religion serving socialism."

Under Xi's presidency, tensions have increased. For example, from 2014 to 2016 the authorities removed crosses from many churches in Zhejiang Province, and some entire churches were demolished. These actions haven't been limited to unregistered churches, as evidenced in the case of the huge TSPM Chongyi Church in Hangzhou, which includes many young professionals, including returnees. Chongyi's senior pastor, Gu Yuese, who had protested the cross removals, was dismissed and arrested—accused of misappropriation of funds.[68]

Some lawyers representing these churches have been arrested. Zhejiang, particularly the city of Wenzhou, has more churches than other provinces. There

---

66 A Google search for "Beijing Shouwang Church" reveals comments about one such church.
67 http://thediplomat.com/2016/08/the-politics-of-religion-in-china/
68 http://www.csw.org.uk/2017/01/13/news/3425/article.htm

is debate as to whether the government will extend such treatment to other provinces.

Nevertheless, political restrictions may not be the only concern for some Chinese churches. Brent Fulton has argued that urbanization, with its massive movement of people, poses the greatest challenge to the Chinese church.[69] In this context, though, churches can shine as beacons of light, bringing a gospel of hope both to the educated middle classes who have found affluence empty and to the marginalized poor migrating to the cities.

One church leader listed five issues facing the church: anti-religious prejudice; mistrust of "alien religions," arising from a revival of Sinology (or Chinese nationalism); the post-modern entertainment culture; liberal social morality; and materialism.[70] We can note that all but the second of these five issues are also applicable outside China. Just a few years ago, one writer suggested the main risks that Chinese Christians feel in relation to pursuing their faith aren't risks to their safety but rather ridicule, missing out financially, and being regarded as different.[71] Hopefully recent events like the clampdown on the use of certain social media won't be the start of long-term increased official constraint on the church.

Opportunities and issues facing returnees in church

Christian students who return to China expecting challenges and then meet those challenges with humility, prayer, and perseverance will find wonderful opportunities to serve in the church. They can also help other returnees settle in and contribute. A few—generally those who have lived abroad long enough to become Christians, grow in their faith, and learn to share and teach the faith to others—have returned to plant churches. Degree programs are shorter in some countries than in others. Master's programs are only one year in the UK, for example, so new believers have less time to become rooted in Christ.

For some returnees, their church abroad represented a place for English-language practice or safe social contact, thus meeting felt needs that no longer exist now they are back home.. Others see no need for church since they now have God, which might have its source in the fact that in China religion traditionally means visiting temples to pay off gods or pray for good fortune. Or such an attitude might arise from the individualism experienced abroad, even in the church. Students may have been taught about the importance of a personal relationship with God but not about the role of the church and why believers need to be together.

Academics, policemen, and government employees—especially those in senior levels—may be wary of revealing their faith by attending church. Many are simply overwhelmed by the combination of work, family, and social pressures that are hard for us to understand in our comparatively relaxed societies. Something that seemed so exciting or romantic abroad may fade when family

---

69   Fulton, *China's Urban Christians*.
70   http://www.chinasource.org/resource-library/chinese-church-voices/5-challenges-facing-churches-in-china
71   Wielander, *Christian Values in Communist China*.

or work demands your attention on Sundays or the only church you know of is over an hour away by public transportation.

Church invisibility is a problem, as even major cities have a small number of registered churches compared to the huge population. Since unregistered churches usually have limited visibility, returnees need contacts and introductions to find them and then to be trusted and accepted by them.

Although big cities tend to have large registered churches, members often leave quickly without stopping to chat; this might be because of the limited time before the next service begins or because of apprehensions arising from past history and the experience of constant surveillance. Getting to know people can be hard. We should encourage returnees to inquire about small groups.

Some returnees are disappointed not to find a church just like their church abroad. Sometimes they struggle with a church's formality, high proportion of older people (usually women), or old-fashioned music. One time I accompanied a returnee on her first visit to church in China. I was quite impressed by the good sermon, the number of young people, and an invitation to a Bible study. But my friend wasn't impressed—essentially because the church was different than her overseas church.

Because some churches are hierarchical, it can take a while for returnees to qualify to serve. And because of the low ratio of pastors to congregants, pastors may have little time to talk to newcomers. They also tend to be wary of returnees with strong opinions. Many returnees have become used to a foreign education style and Bible study leaders who encourage critical thinking and expression of opinions; thus they struggle with how to communicate with Chinese church leaders and find it hard to submit to their authority. Returnees coming from well-established overseas churches may be unaware of the pressures facing young Chinese house church leaders, who may have no elders to consult, no role models, no denominational support to fall back on, and very limited income.

The quality of teaching varies among churches in China, as do the restrictions on teaching. Fortunately, the number of Bible colleges and graduates is growing. A couple of years ago I enjoyed browsing in registered church bookstores in Hangzhou and Ningbo, although I don't know how representative that is of other cities. And China is blessed with Christian literature websites. Though access to certain foreign Christian websites is barred, Chinese Christians maintain a vibrant online presence.

Returnees have told me about constraints in regard to registered churches preaching on certain subjects, such as the second coming of Christ; but later I heard that subject preached in a registered church elsewhere. Some were wary of efforts to use church teaching and activities for political ends. One interviewee commented that in some registered churches the pulpit is used for homilies about being good citizens rather than for its full potential:

The topic they're talking about . . . the teaching . . . is not so deep. Because it's banned to talk about [things] like Jesus Christ's second coming, resurrection; not to emphasize [things] like death, hell, the devil. So it's just encouraging the people to do good things, to be a good person, to be positive . . . not to make any trouble, not to oppose the government.

On the other hand, some students who are already Christians when they leave China find churches abroad strange. Tian was puzzled by the informality of her British church. When I visited her church in China, I could see why. I too had to adjust—to the long service, wearing a head covering, and sitting on the left side with the other women.

Returnees need to be able to discern when rules and traditions are in accordance with biblical teaching and the leading of the Holy Spirit and when they're not, when it's best to stay and when they should move on.

New religious movements, cults, and false teaching

Jehovah's Witnesses and Mormons are active in China. China also has homegrown cults, such as Eastern Lightning (东方闪电; Dōngfāng Shǎndiàn), which is also known as the Church of Almighty God. Members of the group, which has been operating in China for many years, say that Jesus has already returned.[72] One returnee's sister's church was infiltrated by them.

In 2014, people claiming to be from Eastern Lightning beat a woman to death in a McDonalds in Shandong because she refused to give them her phone number. This horrendous crime was broadcast nationwide on Chinese television. Several returnees told me that though most people realize this group has nothing to do with true Christianity, colleagues or family warned them to steer clear of *all* "religion and superstition." Eastern Lightning now operates in several countries and has its own "Scriptures," including *The Word Appears in the Flesh*, along with an English-language presence on YouTube and Facebook.

While the authorities try to eradicate such groups, they must have a hard task identifying which ones really are "evil cults" and which are true Christian house churches. Some officials may well regard all unregistered churches as "evil cults."

China is not free from the prosperity gospel. The traditional Chinese religious emphasis on using prayer and sacrifices to obtain health and wealth likely contributes to the popularity of groups teaching that if you give to the church and have enough faith, God will increase your income. We must help new Christians embrace a theology of suffering and learn to identify true and false teaching, good and bad churches.

---

72   This claim was the headline of a full-page ad placed in the UK newspaper *The Times* on July 12, 2014.

Ready to Serve

When Guang returned to China, he settled into a church quickly, happy to be with Christians who shared the same language and culture. Shared struggles deepened their faith.

Li returned determined to serve. He started attending a registered church; but it was hard to get to know people in the big Sunday service, and the sermons didn't satisfy him since they were aimed at people who were either less educated than him or brand-new Christians. So Li inquired about small groups and joined one. At first he couldn't understand why the group members seemed so serious and not very friendly. But he made an effort to get to know them, particularly the group leader. Eventually Li gained the leader's trust; and the leader explained that because they were wary of cults infiltrating the church, they had to be careful with new people. Li has remained in that church, making a point to welcome newcomers.

Yong joined a house church. Although the teaching wasn't as deep as he was used to and the service times were difficult for his schedule, he made a commitment to stay. He now helps with music and leads a small group. While studying abroad his church provided opportunities to serve; he helped lead missions among Chinese students and invested time and money attending Bible camps and a returnee conference. All that prepared him well.

Some returnees eventually become church leaders, like quiet Xue. In the UK she was encouraged to pray and read the Bible in Chinese; and while there, Xue first tried leading worship.

These four people are all bearing fruit in China; they returned armed and ready for battle.

PART 3
The People

5 Seven Stories

Until now I've used illustrations from many returnees' lives. Now we're going to focus on nineteen who shared with me in depth. Later we'll take a close look at whether, and how, their core values changed. But first I'll introduce you to seven of them more closely.

All nineteen had been postgraduates or visiting scholars (people holding academic posts in Chinese universities). They had all lived abroad for at least one year and said they first believed in Christ abroad. All had been back in China for at least a year, some longer. Fifteen are women and four are men. They lived in seven cities, twelve of them in Beijing and Shanghai, the two cities most popular with returnees.

Some were affluent, by Chinese standards, but not all. When I first met Fuyin, she and her husband were struggling financially, both unemployed. Luli, her husband, and her mother-in-law were living in two rooms, sharing kitchen facilities with other families.

Table 1 presents some basic information about the nineteen returnees I interviewed. I have not used their real names or those of their friends and relatives.

Table 1: Interviewees

Name	M/F	Age	Marital status	Occupation	Study level
Baozhai	F	28	Married; expecting first child	HR manager in international firm	Masters
Changlan	M	29	Married	IT manager in international firm	Masters
Enci	F	29	Single	International trade	Masters
Fuyin	F	38	Married; one child	Seeking paid work	Masters
Guang	M	28	Single	Designer	Masters
Huifang	F	44	Married; one child	University professor	Visiting scholar
Jiang	M	37	Married; one child	Economist	PhD
Jinjing	F	46	Married; one child	University lecturer	Visiting scholar
Ling	F	26	Single	Engineer	Masters
Luli	F	33	Married; expecting first child	HR consultant	Masters
Mingzhu	F	46	Married	University professor	PhD
Qingzhao	F	30	Married; one child	English teacher	Masters
Ruolan	F	39	Married; one child	University lecturer	PhD
Song	F	26	Married	Financial services	Masters
Xiaodan	F	33	Married	Part-time administrator	Masters
Xifeng	F	28	Single	Charity worker	Masters
Xing	M	33	Married; one child	Lawyer	Masters
Xue	F	34	Single	Government administrator	Masters
Yan	F	33	Married; three children	Childcare; part-time work	Masters

Xue: A Dream to Serve a King

When I first met Xue in China in 2009 she was thirty-four, single, an only child, and had been back six years. She had spent two years in the UK as a postgraduate. She hesitated to meet me at first because she was busy with work, church responsibilities, and a course related to her Christian ministry. She was active and fulfilled, but had not always been so.

A lonely childhood

When I asked her to describe her childhood, Xue replied:

> I should say loneliness. Yeah, because my parents are quite busy at work, so I always feel by myself, I mean in a spiritual way. They take care of me, I don't lack anything, but in a spiritual way—like life guidance—my parents cannot give me a lot of support. So yeah, that's the childhood memory.

Xue's father had a government job, enabling him to provide a good education and everything she needed materially, but he did not express emotions. Xue felt that her schoolteacher mother treated her like one of her pupils. Relatives' comments that Xue was not pretty led her to make unfavorable comparisons between herself and her "beautiful" cousins. She even wondered for a while if she was adopted.

Xue's happiest memory of her schooldays was of regularly scoring the highest mark in history and literature. She was influenced by the kind father of a schoolmate, who was like an uncle to her. He would talk with them about literature and philosophy, encouraging Xue's interest.

Early searches for truth

Although this "uncle" had a Bible on his bookshelf, they didn't discuss it, and Xue wasn't aware of meeting any Christians in her teenage years. Sometimes she listened to Buddhist music or went to a temple, out of curiosity. She was interested in what lies beyond the material world. Laughing, she said:

> I always thought I was from another planet. I was always chatting with the stars when I was little, because I was always by myself. So during the night I spoke to the stars.

At university, Xue took opportunities to go to lectures on a variety of topics, including one about Daoism. That lecture left a deep impression, but she concluded that Daoism "is not a real truth." One time she responded to an advertisement encouraging students to write to an address in Germany to receive free books. The books arrived, but she never read them; looking back, she thinks they were about Christianity.

Before studying abroad Xue had never been to a church, although she had wanted to.

I tried to find people going to church during Christmas, but they described it to me and I thought, "That's not what I'm looking for"—You know, crowded with people and they just want blessings or something like that.

Xue read classic Chinese novels as a girl and thinks that these stimulated her early admiration for the courtly life; she was impressed with the idea of being a servant to a great king. As she grew up, she realized:

Oh, there are no kings, so how can I do it? I thought, "Maybe I'll be a secretary to a director of a company." I almost forgot that when I got a job, you know, graduated from university; and then I remembered it when I became a Christian. I remember I always had this kind of ambition.

Undergraduate life

Xue studied languages at university. She enjoyed this and was top of her class. Her teachers appreciated her ability and interest in their subject. However, things became less happy as graduation approached. There was fierce competition among classmates for scarce jobs in their field. Students who had been nice before now seemed to distrust Xue and even started rumors about her. Although the teachers stood by her, it made her wary of other people's motives and less confident socially.

I think about all the academic things I can do very well, but in society I'm not very good at how to deal with different people and deal with difficult situations.

First job and father's influence

Although Xue's father was distant emotionally, he exerted strong influence. He ensured that she went to a top high school; then his intervention led her to a top university's language program—as opposed to history, which was her real interest. After graduation Xue had a successful interview for a job that would have led to an academic career. She felt well suited for the job and was excited about it. But her father didn't think it would pay well enough, so he found her an administrative job in a government department. The feeling of being a misfit in this kind of work remained with her.

Xue said that some things in her life were "very Chinese style." She was referring to her father's repeated interventions. Since she had wanted to get a job by herself, she was ashamed that she had relied on her father. She described how he was still intervening, in marriage and money matters. But this was after she became a Christian, and she had a rather different response. More about that later.

Xue's first job lasted three years and included working in a rural area of China for a while. She enjoyed the chance to work outdoors and to have more spare time than frenetic big-city life afforded. Then her father intervened again, negotiating a chance for her to go to the UK for a year to study English.

I think you will realize that so far my father made every decision for me in my life. He created this opportunity for me, so I had no choice.

First trip abroad: "I will find the purpose of my life"

Her two years abroad were "the happiest time" of Xue's life to that point. She felt comfortable there; the people were friendly and she liked their lifestyle. Although she lived in a city that was quite large by local standards, compared to China it was "a quiet country life; not much entertainment, just simple and quiet." When Xue arrived, her first thought was:

> This is the first time in my life that I can control everything by myself. I have freedom!

During her first year, Xue just did an English course. This gave her time to explore what her host city had to offer and travel to other places. Soon after her arrival, two Singaporean students approached her and asked if she was a newcomer and would like to join a city tour they were organizing. That was the start of her contact with Christians.

These new friends invited Xue to Globe Café, where a group of people, both international and British, met one evening a week in a church building. She enjoyed the conversations and the occasional short talks. What these people didn't know is that before she left China, Xue had written on a piece of paper, "What I will do in England: I will find the purpose of my life."

When she was invited to join a weekly Bible study group, Xue accepted immediately. The group was led by a local Christian; the others were all Chinese students who were not Christians. They were reading Genesis. Unfortunately, this experience was disappointing to Xue. The other Chinese were asking questions related to science and evolution, but that didn't interest Xue. Since childhood she had already believed in the existence of an overall God.

Xue became frustrated that her own questions were not being answered. One thing, however, kept her from dropping out: initially she thought the group leader wasn't very smart because his answers weren't always convincing; but she became impressed by his kindness—for example, to give people a ride home. Although Xue still didn't believe what he was saying,

> I just could see in his eyes that he had some enthusiasm, and I started thinking, "Why does this man trust his God so much?"

When this course was over, someone who had heard about Xue's frustration with it arranged for her to meet an English Christian young woman one on one. They talked about topics from the Bible that interested Xue.

At an international student weekend away, another Chinese student recommended the book *Yóuzǐ Yín* (遊子吟, *Song of a Wanderer*), written by Li Cheng. A particular passage struck Xue. It said something like, "You can pray to God. If he is not true, you lose nothing. But if he is true, you gain a lot." She pondered on this, though it all still seemed a bit unreal. She started asking Christians to tell her their stories, questioning them avidly.

Nine months after arriving in the UK, Xue asked a Chinese Christian whether God chooses people. The young woman replied, "Yes, I was chosen." Xue felt so sad:

I thought, "I'm nothing special at all; God will not choose me."

Just after that, someone else visited Xue, and she described her sadness. Her friend asked, "What do you believe?"

> I said, "I believe I'm a sinner, and I trust in Jesus"—something like that. She said, "I think you are a Christian." I said, "Oh, that simple?"

The next day, Xue prayed, "God, if you are true, please show me." Immediately she opened her Bible and her eyes fell upon Matthew 7:7: "Knock and the door will be opened to you." Soon afterward Xue returned to China, without telling anyone in the UK what had happened.

Back in China: God answers prayer

Having spent one year in England, Xue hoped to return for a second year to work on her master's degree. She was offered a place in a university in another city, and money wasn't a problem. However, she discovered that there wasn't enough time to go through the visa process. Though her plan to return to England seemed impossible, Xue prayed, "Oh God, if you want me to go to England, then help me." She immediately felt at peace. The visa was granted with unusual speed. This time her heavenly Father, not her earthly father, intervened on her behalf.

Second UK stay: "I'm a Christian"

On Xue's very first day back in the UK, in a new city where she knew no one, a South Asian student living next door came to say hello. When she told Xue she was a Christian, Xue replied, "I'm a Christian too." This was the first time she had said this about herself out loud. She had a new self-concept.

Xue's new neighbor invited her to church; and there she met people who helped her "grow up": a pastor and other international student Christians, including a Taiwanese girl who spoke Chinese. These new friends encouraged Xue to read the Bible and pray in Chinese, which would prove to be a great help to her. She described that year as "full of God's grace."

At first the local British students in her program weren't friendly; one pointedly ignored her. Xue thought it must be because her English and academic performance were poor. She prayed, persevered with her work, and the other students' attitudes changed; the difficult one even started talking to her. When academic work became a struggle, Xue prayed and received God's help. She got good grades, earned her degree, and returned to China.

China again: Finding a church

Back home, Xue didn't know how to find a church. She commented that God helped her because she helped someone else—a foreigner needing help to make a purchase. When Xue went to the shop with her, she noticed a wall hanging with words from the Bible on it. The shop owner was a Christian and invited Xue to his church.

Xue found this house church to be very different than what she was hoping for. The people were older than her and from a different background.

They were not very educated and they didn't have a pastor; they just shared their experiences on Sunday. You know, someone gets something and they think it's from God and they talk about it. But in that church there's a good thing: They think everyone should serve ... everyone should clean or wash up or something. Yes, everyone should serve; that's very good. They really have a good heart to serve, but they don't have a lot of knowledge. So I thought I was quite different from people there.

It helped that Xue was familiar with praying in Chinese, happy to use a Chinese Bible, and had no fixed notion of the form church should take. Not long after this, friends in the UK told Xue about a fellowship in her city for new Christian returnees from the UK. She settled well in this group.

Eventually Xue left the first church because of time constraints. But in the fellowship Xue grew in faith and knowledge of the Bible and took opportunities to serve. Eventually the leaders introduced her to another house church, which was comprised of professional people like herself.

Over the years, Xue has accepted various roles and responsibilities in the church. When I met her, six years after her return to China, she was an elder and also helping with the returnee fellowship. At thirty-four, she was one of the oldest members of the church. She was also involved in work supportive of the wider church. She was feeling rather overburdened and considering whether she should give something up.

I have stayed in touch with Xue and know that her energetic commitment to wise church leadership has not waned. She has stepped down from returnee ministry to focus on church responsibilities. She sees the people at church as her family.

Parents: Pressure to marry

When Xue returned to China she was twenty-eight, past the age when Chinese daughters are expected to be married. Like many Chinese parents, hers arranged dates for her with men they considered suitable marriage prospects. Xue made it clear that she wished only to marry a Christian, but as an obedient daughter she agreed to the arranged dates, despite the men not being Christians. Laughing, she explained:

> Actually, I just accepted because I thought I could talk with them about the Bible, but I failed in both ways!

When I first met Xue she had been adopting this approach for six years. She continued for several more years, coping also with the awareness that colleagues and acquaintances held the common view that someone unmarried at her age must be a bit strange. Recently, after putting up with her parents' dating arrangements for ten years, she met and married a Christian man in her church. Even that wasn't straightforward; while her parents were happy with the arrangement, his, initially, were not. Now she has someone with whom she can serve God. Ever since her return Xue had hoped that one day she would marry and serve with her husband in church.

A few years ago, when she was still single, Xue's father committed her to buying a flat, and to paying a mortgage, without consulting her first. He explained that since she appeared not to be planning her life, he should plan it for her. Initially she was angry, but after a while—seeing his disappointment—she wrote to him, acknowledging his concern for her. Now that Xue is married she should be free of some of the pressure that comes with having to accept her father's help; she thinks her father will see his responsibility for her as having passed to her husband.

New identity: A precious child of God

In the past Xue constantly worried about what her father thought. Now, as a maturing Christian, this pressure was lifting:

> Before, I felt pressure that I should please him. And also I always feel that I'm nothing good before him. But now I think I have special value, separate from him.

Previously Xue had also worried about what would become of her if anything happened to her father. How would she manage?

> It's complicated. Because he makes all the decisions, sometimes I worry that if he is not here, what should I do? Because I never tried to live without him, I was always worrying about him. But now I think, "No, God's in control; and God also has control over him."

Before believing in Christ, Xue had no plans because her father decided everything. She just imagined life would continue in the same way. Now she was experiencing God being in control. She gave an example. She had been thinking about going to theological college, then probably getting married, and then working full time in the church with her future husband. She called this her "reasonable dream"; she was so bored in her job, doing the same mundane work for years. She now thought, however, that God had closed the door on this dream and wanted her to remain in her job.

Xue felt that her relationship with God varied. Two years earlier it had been very close; her Bible reading highlighted verses that seemed very helpful and she felt clear about God's plan for her. When we met, she was doing more in the church and supporting others more, but she felt somewhat distant from God; she could see him at work, but it was "not so sweet like before." She compared it to a romantic relationship with a boy: "At first you're very close, and now you just get into normal life."

Specifically, Xue felt that she now respected God more but was less emotional. Initially she had been so overjoyed at his love for her that maybe she had not "really put effort into knowing what God is like." She thought she occasionally misinterpreted God because of her experience with her own earthly father; she sometimes expected God to be harsh with her because her father had been.

Despite occasional dips in her *feelings* about God, Xue now has a very different self-concept than she did when she was younger. Instead of feeling like an unwanted outsider, she knows that she is loved and valued by her eternal Father, who has a purpose for her, and that she is a valued member of a church family where she can serve the King.

Adopted into the family

One of the biggest changes in Xue's life, since starting to follow Christ, was that she had close relationships with her church "brothers and sisters," with whom she shared common aims, values, and interests.

Xue spent nearly all her time outside of work in church relationships and activities, including taking a Christian counseling course and translating books. She found that she had abilities and gifts she never knew about before.

> I find that I can do something, you know. Before I think I can't do anything good, but now I can do something. I translate books, chat with people, and lead Bible study. I can't imagine that before.

The workplace

Xue's fulfilling church life has not been without cost. She has had the same relatively junior secular administrative job for years. It is below her ability and quite tedious. However, it leaves her with time and energy that a more interesting, senior job would not.

And over the years, Xue's desire to act in a way that pleases God, in accordance with biblical teaching, has sometimes made her unpopular with bosses and colleagues. Because of a problem with senior management, she was denied a promotion. Her refusal to collude in a tax-avoidance scheme annoyed some colleagues and was perhaps shaming for them.

Not wandering anymore

Xue's perception of the world, people, and her own value, purpose, and destiny changed utterly. She went to the UK looking for her purpose in life. Six years after her return, she had a new identify: as a child of God with a new family, her church. She was no longer searching.

> Before, I was just reading books and looking for the truth. But now I know the truth, so I will never want to look for things. So that's a big change.

Previously, Xue had gone along with the widespread view that acquiring material goods and status is what matters.

> Before, I think my focus should be getting all the good things people think is good—you know, house, money. Although I don't [have] interest in those things, everyone thinks they're very important; so I think getting more of these kind of things is good. But now I think God made me in this world, must have some purpose, so just do that purpose. That's what I think is important. I've found my value in doing God's work.

Xue also said that it was important to her to be valued by others, not for her status beauty, or cleverness—but simply for herself.

Xue's mother and old friends can see that she has changed. They say she is more confident, not easily becoming nervous or depressed. She helps them rather than being shut away in her own private world. Although Xue was once fearful, or critical, of people, she says that the Bible helps her understand their motives better.

> I think the Bible is a clear book about the nature of people. And now I can understand why I can't get on well with other people, what the problem is between us. Yes, I think this is a big change. I think I can be more tolerant and patient with other people than before. I'm not always thinking other people hurt me. I think they just don't know what they do.

When asked about the benefits of being a Christian, Xue replied:

> Hope. Eternal life. Yeah, I think there's a lot of things, gifts from God. But what most attracts me is future: the eternal life and the hope. Yeah, that more attracts me. Also, I'm not lonely; although sometimes I feel lonely—but not really lonely as before. I have many friends and I have things to do in my life. I'm not wandering.

Fuyin: The End of a Human Is the Beginning of God

The woman sitting opposite me in a quiet corner of a Beijing restaurant was radiant. As she told me what had happened since we met four years earlier, in Beijing in 2009, I was stunned at what she and her family had been through, yet delighted at the change in her. She was free in Christ. But that was not the case when I met her the first time and she told me her story. Then she had been back in China for over two years and a Christian for almost the same time, but I had sensed disappointment rankling. Now she was clear in her purpose and had a revolutionized life.

Childhood: The desire to excel and to be loved and valued

When we met in 2009, I was immediately struck by two things: her choice of the name Fuyin as her alias for my research, and her immediate declaration that her parents had greatly affected her life. *Fuyin* (福音, *Fú yīn*) is the Chinese word for "gospel."

Fuyin grew up in a northern provincial capital, in a household in which both parents were highly competitive and quick to anger. Fuyin's father was fifty-three when she was born in 1971, the youngest of three sisters. Disappointed that his first child was a girl, he didn't attend the births of the next two. His disappointment at having no son added to Fuyin's feeling of being unloved.

Fuyin attributed her father's temper to his joining the army at fourteen and fighting in the war against Japan and in the civil war (1945–1949). She recalled waiting in fear for her parents to return home from their work as hospital doctors, knowing that if they had had a bad day the children could be in for a beating. Even her efforts to please her parents by being first in her class didn't seem to help. Academic success, teachers' praise, and a position as monitor gave her some comfort and sense of worth in primary school.

With a breaking voice, Fuyin described her teenage years as a lonely time of not being understood by adults or peers. In her isolation, she turned to writing; the only happy memory of those years was having an article published. At seventeen she met Long, the boy who later became her husband. Although it was a relief to have someone consistently caring for her, she said the distraction of this relationship caused her to fail the all-important university entrance exam.

Like most schoolchildren of her era, Fuyin did not choose her field. She went to banking school, despite her love of language and literature.

> I personally wanted to be a teacher, but my parents said, "You can't make a lot of money. You have to move on to the financial side." So they sent me to banking school. In our culture our future is normally decided by our parents; you can't have your own opinion. "I want to be . . ." No, no. We don't have the right to decide our future. Always have to follow what parents ask you to do. Otherwise, you're not a good child."

This led to a high-paying but stressful job in an insurance company. Outside of work, Fuyin studied for a degree in English literature, as a degree was required for higher paying, more senior jobs. She said all three sisters inherited from their parents the desire to be the best, which stayed with her into adult life.

> It was very, very tiring for me, because I feel I want to be the best, so I had to pay double efforts, or sometimes even more, to get what I want. (She laughs.) It was very tiring.

Fuyin lived with her parents while she was in school. The atmosphere was even more tense because, by not getting into a "proper" university, she failed in her filial responsibility to give her parents face. At age twenty-four, she married and moved away from the parents she "hated."

Early married years
Fuyin described meeting and marrying Long as the only bright point in her life prior to her conversion. She recalled the early years of their marriage, contrasting it with life with her parents:

> Long was very caring. Always cared about me, made me feel comfortable; at least he understood me, cared about me. He didn't beat me; that for me was valuable, because I hated my parents the way they treated us. I expected I would marry a person who loved me; that's enough. Only love me, give me a very peaceful life. That's all. I didn't expect him to make a lot of money, because I did. Working in an insurance company makes a lot of money.

Work: Seeking recognition and sincerity
Fuyin despised the expectation of bribery and flattering the boss. She wanted to be rewarded for ability or good work. She placed high value on achieving her full potential on her own merit. She credited her father's teaching with her aversion to flattery.

She stayed with the insurance company for eleven years, even though she hated having to beg all her connections to buy insurance from her in order to hit the high sales targets. Despite eventually being promoted to a managerial position, Fuyin "felt empty inside." She heard of someone who had gone to study abroad and thought, "If she can do it, why not me?" So, selling her house and using her parents' savings and money from a wealthy in-law, she set off abroad in September of 2002. She believed studying abroad would provide the knowledge and qualifications to get a better job, which would "release her potential," either in China or abroad—where she believed work relationships were "easier" and the work environment more "pure."

It was also important to her to be seen to have achieved. Getting a job abroad before returning to China would give her face upon her return. Later, failing in this aim was "a great blow."

The UK: Difficulties and misunderstanding

Fuyin arrived in the UK to find that the university she had chosen was not as good as she thought. So she returned home, to Long and their young son, and applied to a better university. However, when she returned to the UK in August of 2003, because of an error there was no place in the university for her; she would have to wait until the autumn of 2004. Unable to start the master's program and unable to work full time on a student visa, she was devastated. Her hopes were in tatters. But she picked herself up and started studying part-time at a local college.

Fuyin met a Singaporean lady at the bus stop who invited Fuyin to her home. There she met local Christians who read the Bible and prayed for each other. Although Fuyin wasn't very interested in the Bible, she was lonely and the people were kind; so she continued going to the Bible study and also joined them at church. She stopped going when her family arrived, her new program started, and she became too busy for Christian activities.

About this time, problems arose in the family. Marital tension developed to the extent that Fuyin seriously considered divorcing Long. Throughout their marriage, he never had a stable job and she had always been the main breadwinner. Now money was running out. She tried working part-time in a fast-food restaurant, but she quit because it was very tiring and she felt she lost too much face doing that kind of job. The importance she attached to working hard to achieve her potential added to the frustration she felt with her husband, who lacked the confidence, language skills, and energy to find a job.

> I made up my mind twice to divorce him. I can't live with that kind of man: no responsibility; just wait, wait, wait; very reactive, not proactive. I'm very proactive.

Meanwhile, Fuyin's intermittent contact with Christian locals continued. A misunderstanding developed, though, because they thought Fuyin had become a Christian and she had not. When she was deciding whether to look for work in the UK or China after graduation, they advised her to pray for God's guidance; but relating Christian belief to getting a job seemed crazy to Fuyin.

> At that time I didn't believe, so I thought it was extremely funny. "It's OK if I go to church or I make Christian friends or I attend the Bible study group or house group, but it has nothing to do with my work." I couldn't relate it, associate the two together. So I thought, "That's really silly." I replied to him very politely. "OK, I will think about it." But I just dropped it. For me it was nonsense.

Crisis

Fuyin hoped to work abroad before returning home. This would give her valuable experience and solve her pressing financial problems. Also, failing to get a job abroad would mean loss of face—for her and her family. However, despite obtaining a highly skilled migrant visa, she couldn't get a job. This, combined with disappointment in her marriage, led to a crisis and the turning point in Fuyin's story. She no longer felt able to control her own life.

Reflecting on this time, Fuyin quoted a Chinese Christian saying: "The end of a human being is the beginning of God." She sighed and then said:

> That was another hit, a blow. So at that time, September, I remember very clearly, just right in that month, I believed in God. I just found I was making effort toward that direction (indicating left). But God, although I didn't believe in him at that time (laughing) . . . There was an invisible power leading me to that direction (indicating right), just completely different. And also that power was much, much, much higher than mine, so I just felt I was useless; I didn't know what to do. I was [always] full of energy, but suddenly I was just completely empty and very, very tired. I didn't know where to go and how I should do the next step in my life.

Looking back, Fuyin saw the UK job-hunting period as a significant time:

> That year was really important in my believing in God. Then I was a person kind of proud of myself. Whenever I decided to do something, I could always make it; so it really made me very proud of my ability. I had the work experience and a UK certificate, so I was pretty confident of getting a job in the UK. But after nearly half a year I got nothing.

Then Fuyin and Long watched a Christian DVD sent by a Chinese friend in Australia. They were shocked by how reasonable the arguments sounded. Both of them decided to believe in God. Suddenly they felt at peace and agreed that if the next job interview failed they would return to China, as that would mean God wanted them to return. At that point, Fuyin said, they didn't understand about Jesus and salvation, but just believed in God's existence.

> I decided to accept God, but it was two steps. First, for Chinese people it's very hard to acknowledge the existence of God, because it's invisible. A lot of people say, "I won't believe what I don't see." So at that time it was the first step in my life: I accept there is a God existing in the universe. Although I don't know where he is, but I decided to accept him; and so did my husband. So, in September, we both believed. It's very, very clear in my mind. We didn't get baptized, but it's definite we believed, because there was a sign— we suddenly felt peaceful.

Just before this, Fuyin had been meeting with a Jehovah's Witness, because the girl persisted and was nice, and Fuyin felt sorry for her. She challenged the Witness to justify her belief in this invisible God and in the Bible. The Witness gave her a book describing archaeological evidence for the historicity of the Bible. This contributed to her positive reaction to the Christian DVD. From that point Fuyin started reading the Bible closely, remembered prior warnings about Jehovah's Witnesses and stopped meeting with them, and went back to church. She also started reading the Bible with a local Christian she had met earlier. Shortly afterward, upon returning to China in 2007, listening to online sermons, and talking with Christians, Fuyin's faith developed to include belief in salvation through Christ.

During her former life in China, Fuyin had never really considered religion. As a child she visited a famous mountain, popular with Buddhists, and had seen other children's parents burn incense. Long's grandmother owned a Bible, but never mentioned anything about Christianity. Fuyin accepted the standard teaching of communism that there is only a physical world and no God.

Back in China: Under new authority

The Fuyin I met in 2009 clearly had a very different worldview than the Fuyin who first went abroad. She had a new master story and self-concept, which she lived out. This narrative included a God who intervenes personally in her life. She commented that God "led" her back to Beijing rather than Shanghai and that she received "reassurance from God" when she read Christian literature.

Fuyin frequently referred to God speaking to her personally: during church sermons, after praying, or when reading the Bible. Her descriptions of two incidents related to her husband provide examples. One day in the UK, after praying, she heard a voice, which she believed to be God's, say, "Love your husband." And then one day after they returned to China, and Long was still unemployed, he was giving her a ride on his bicycle.

> I sat behind him, and suddenly I realized I was only focusing on his negative side. I didn't realize how good he was treating me and my family and my son, all sorts of things. And suddenly I, in tears (her voice breaks), said to him, "God gave you to me and I didn't realize how good you are. I always just found your negative side."

Back in China, Fuyin worked for another insurance company but found she couldn't promote products as persuasively as before. Talking about the Christian gospel came naturally, but when she spoke about insurance she felt "disappointed." Sharing the gospel was so important to her that she carried leaflets to give to people who might be interested. She showed me some she had with her.

Life in China was hard. The insurance job did not satisfy her; some colleagues were jealous of her overseas degree; her husband was unemployed; their standard of living was lower than before she went abroad. But despite the daily struggles, she knew God was leading them.

Fuyin said that she is very much a "work in progress." She looked back on herself, as a new Christian, talking about the Bible with women at work, women she struggled to get along with. She said of that former self: "I was very proud."

A new family life

Initially Fuyin's parents wanted to hear about God and seemed to believe. They could see the difference in their daughter. Gradually, though, they returned to their old ways, quarreling with and criticizing Fuyin for her faith. For example, one day after she gave thanks for a meal, her father said, "I bought this food for you, not God. If he can give you food from heaven, just let him drop the food for you."

Fuyin was sad that her parents' marriage was so unhappy and they couldn't get beyond the idea that if God existed he would automatically provide a high-paying job. Nonetheless, she told me that despite having had "great hatred" for her parents, God's love for her and the peace he gave her enabled her to forgive them for beating her as a child. The hatred was gone.

A radical change had taken place in her marriage. Twice, once abroad and once in China, God intervened to stop her from divorcing Long. Her son had noticed the difference too. He said, "Mum, you've changed." Previously she had been quick to scold him; now she was calmer and more reasonable.

Trusting God: Unemployment struggles

When I met Fuyin in 2009, neither she nor Long was in paid work. She had left the insurance company to work for a man who claimed to be a Christian; but because his actions suggested otherwise, she left. She was praying and looking for a new job, while leading a Bible study and teaching neighborhood children English. The family's money had almost run out. Life required great perseverance, but Fuyin said she had God's peace and knew he was in control.

Several times Fuyin mentioned expecting God to "use" her, once quoting from Mother Teresa about being a pencil in God's hand. She referred to the Bible, to incidents in the lives of Jacob and Abraham, as she described seeking to find out what God wanted her to do. In sharing about the peace God had given her, Fuyin referred to verses in Romans regarding examples of people trusting God in times of difficulty, waiting for God to act rather than depending on their own actions. Trusting God and doing what he wants was clearly important to Fuyin. Describing her reaction to a sermon about Christ's crucifixion, she said:

> I was in tears seven days. After that I felt . . . I was completely transformed by God. Completely it's a new me. And the old me just, yeah, simply gone; and I felt I am a servant for him, not me. I couldn't not care about others— always doing things for others, just very naturally. It's nothing from my side. And I decided, I prayed to God, to live a holy life.

Trusting God to look after her and the family was a source of both comfort and tension. Fuyin's idea that she could run her own business teaching children English, and then introduce their parents to Christ, gave her comfort that she would have both an income and a way of serving God. However, this idea was in tension with other feelings that she could "do more" with her talents and experience, and also ran counter to her Long's comments that she could do something more prestigious.

A Biblical worldview

Fuyin repeatedly talked about God acting in her life. She had her Bible with her, and referred to passages that had helped her. She identified with people in the Bible. She was praising God for his goodness, even in difficulties, and seeking his direction. She was ready and willing to share the gospel.

At that point Fuyin's family was attending a large registered church. She described how God spoke to her through the sermons:

> Nearly every Sunday, I can hear from God, talking to us. That's really like a treasure, very precious. Nearly every week I go to church and I was in tears, because definitely, very clearly, I know that was from God and he especially speak to me.

Fuyin also listened to online sermons. She asked me to recommend those of Tang Chongrong (Stephen Tong), a famous Chinese Indonesian preacher.

Once when Fuyin was praying, in tears, for God to take her to heaven, she heard: "I haven't used you yet." Long was there, so she asked him if he had spoken. He had not. She turned back to prayer, asked for God's comfort, and experienced "a big release" and a conviction that God would lead her to a situation where she would glorify him. Another time God told her she must wait. She reflected: "Waiting is also a kind of worshiping him."

Fuyin's values had changed from seeking respect for excelling, maximizing her career potential, and protecting her family's face to patiently trusting God, sharing the gospel with others, and appreciating her family. The crisis abroad shattered her self-concept as a strong provider and made her open to a new worldview and values. This led her into new relationships: with God, in the church in China, and in a changed relationship with her family.

Transformation

As soon as I met Fuyin again, in 2013, I knew she was different. Her smile was bright and she linked arms with me warmly as we walked along the street. It was as if a burden had been lifted; the slight air of resentment and disappointment, which she had in 2009, was gone. "You won't believe what has happened since I last saw you!" she exclaimed. "It all started shortly after we met last time."

Back then, in 2009, Fuyin and Long were both pretty much unemployed. Now she was working full time for a Christian organization that trains churches how to help parents bring up their children and how to share the gospel with children. Long was a volunteer in the same ministry; she had just dropped him off at the airport to fly to another city to lead a training session. This was the man who, for so long, seemed too timid to work at all! Clearly much had changed in four years. Fuyin explained that only now were they equipped to do this work; only now, after the experiences God had given them in the last four years. He had taught them to trust him.

Late in 2009, Long took a business opportunity. Some of his associates turned out to be less than ethical, and he was duped into getting involved in something very dubious. He became the scapegoat and ended up in prison for ten months—far away from his family, who could only see him occasionally.

This was a period of great testing. Fuyin's son really struggled in his faith. Now, Fuyin said, he was doing well. She had taught him to pray, read the Bible, and take his problems to God. At school, his quiet good behavior and commitment to study caused him to stand out; and the school had recently invited his father to give a parenting talk to other parents.

For Fuyin, the ten months were desperate. She had no job, was concerned about her son, and had little idea how her husband was being treated. She prayed every day for his physical and spiritual health. With Long in prison, so-called friends at church turned away from her. She said she thought now that these people weren't really following Christ, but just going through the motions. She moved to another church and then, later, to yet another (where they were now happily settled). God literally brought Fuyin to her knees. She learned to trust God rather than her own ability. She said God humbled her, made her less judgmental, and gave her the ability to love people. I believed her; it was obvious.

God also changed Fuyin's marriage. When Long was released from prison, he told her that another prisoner—a powerful man whom the other prisoners respected—had taken a liking to him. This man made sure that Long was safe from dangerous prisoners and even had some good food occasionally. Laughing, Fuyin said, "All the time I was praying for his health, he was eating better than we were!"

Also, in his own "roundabout, relational" way, Long shared the gospel with some other prisoners. Fuyin had always used a very direct approach in sharing the gospel, but now she learned from Long that there are different ways. She said she now respects him and treats him as the head of the family.

Eleven years passed between Fuyin's first trip to the UK and our 2013 meeting in China. So much had changed, and I'm sure God hasn't finished shaping her yet!

Fuyin's conversion, or turning to Christ, has taken place over time, in different places and situations, and with ups and downs. The change has been radical: from seeing herself in a heartless, tough world, and feeling desperate for love and respect; to inhabiting a world with a loving God at the center, whom she knows, trusts, and lives to serve. Her prior self-centeredness and critical suspicion of others has turned into concern for others to know the truth and love she knows.

Changlan: "It's Not All about Me!"

When I met Changlan, five years after his return to China, he lived in a large coastal city in Southern China. He was twenty-nine, working as a manager in a multinational company, and had recently married. The pseudonym he chose, *cháng lán* (常 蓝), means "always blue." He explained that it was part of a Christian book title and referred to a clear, blue sky.

A Contrast: Before school and at school

I asked all the interviewees to imagine their life as a story or book and divide it into chapters. Changlan specified only four chapters, but dedicated one to his life before starting school. He explained this emphasis on his earliest years by saying he had warm memories of the love he received from the adults around him then, which contrasted sharply with his experience after starting school. The one-child policy had just been implemented and his parents' and grandparents' entire focus was on him:

> I was surrounded by elders who cared for me. I felt warm love from them. Still I can remember their touches on my head and on my back. It's the first time I ever felt my existence is important to someone else.

This changed after Changlan started school. At the heart of the change were his parents' demands for good results in a school system that he found restrictive and uninteresting. At primary school, bored by requirements to repeat political propaganda, he would fall asleep or talk to friends. This led to beatings from his father and a growing resentment toward him.

> In primary school I thought my parents were my enemies. They are not defending me! They just keep asking for something from me ... to do more, to make them proud.

It was only later, after Changlan went to study abroad and became a Christian, that he started to understand his parents' behavior toward him as a child. By that time he had access to books about the Cultural Revolution that he had not seen in China, and a more critical view of his own behavior, arising from his Christian view of himself as a sinner.

Changlan's father was eleven when the Cultural Revolution broke out in 1966. All aspects of life, including the education system, experienced huge disruption for the next several years. Many schools closed for long periods; Changlan's father's schooling stopped when he was eleven. This led to a life of hard, menial work in restaurants. He was desperate for his son to have all the opportunities that he had not. The beatings Changlan remembered arose from his father's anxiety about him performing well in primary school so that he could go to a good middle school, high school, and university. This would require success in highly competitive exams.

Two of Changlan's core values developed from these early days: having intellectual stimulation and the freedom to explore ideas, and having a good relationship with his parents.

Changlan's relationship with his parents improved somewhat during his later school years. He started to read widely in areas that interested him, despite the directive nature of the education system. However, his university entrance exam score wasn't high enough for him to study the subject he wanted at a prestigious university in a city away from home. Instead, he had to study finance in his home city.

Undergraduate days: Religion? A "fairy tale"

Changlan's disappointment with formal education continued as an undergraduate, so he spent time on his own curriculum: reading widely in literature, history, politics, and natural science; watching foreign films; and meeting foreign students at his university.

> I was very interested in the world outside China. I don't know why. When I was very little I felt I was different from others because my eyes were always looking ahead, not around the city or not even in China. I want to know what in the world is actually happening.

At that point Changlan's experience of religion was limited to his grandmother's ancestor worship and kowtowing to Buddhist idols, and school teaching about atheism and evolution. He had "a very clear mind that there was no God or any kind of religious stuff," and had been taught that he should rely only on himself. He saw the brief extracts of the Bible that he encountered in English-language textbooks as "some legend or fairy tale," and paid them little attention. Even later, in the UK, when other international students suggested he go with them to meet friendly people who discussed the Bible, he had no idea what churches were like; he thought going to church was no different than the way some Chinese people went to temples.

During university, Changlan lived with his parents. Tensions eased. With his parents' encouragement and financial support, he pursued his desire to explore the wider world by going abroad for a master's program.

New community and worldview

Living in university housing with younger local students, who seemed preoccupied with drinking and parties, Changlan initially was very lonely. This was made worse by the fact that he had broken up with his girlfriend just before he left China. Eventually he made friends with some East Asian classmates, including a Chinese woman, Yin, who would later become his wife.

A Japanese friend introduced Changlan to a mixed group of local and East Asian students who were reading John's Gospel. Changlan found the subject interesting, and he enjoyed getting to know people. This led him to begin going first to a local church and then to the Chinese church Yin had started attending. Here, among people who spoke his own language, Changlan acquired a circle of friends; his previously lonely life took on color. Five years after returning to China, he was still in touch with friends he made abroad.

Changlan had not been impressed by everyone who tried to share their faith with him. Jehovah's Witnesses he met on the street, and some Christians, were too pushy. He offered some advice:

> When people try to do it that way, Chinese people will think, "You're so arrogant. How can you be so proud of your Christianity? We have Buddhism and Confucianism. Do I have to commit with you?" Although they smile and say, "OK, yes, yes," actually, in their heart they are not obedient to that.

After fifteen months abroad, the last nine months considering the Bible and Christianity, Changlan committed to following Christ. He described this decision as seeming entirely natural:

> It just came to my mind that I believe in this. It is true and it is good. It is the way it should be.

Without an intellectual or emotional struggle, Changlan experienced a sense of recognizing God:

> I believe that when people believe, not because they are convinced to, it's because it's the right thing to do—just like looking for your father. It's not that you are told, "This is your father." It's that you believe he is; and "It's true!" That's it. I never test my brother that I am the son of my father; but I believe he is my father. That's it; simple as that. You don't have to do the gene test.

Changlan had a new worldview; at the center was a God he had not previously thought existed, but whom he now saw as his ultimate Father. He saw himself differently, as one who had been estranged from God but could now call him Father because of Christ's actions. He had a new explanation of human life and his role in it, especially of himself in relation to God.

Changlan told his father about his decision to become a Christian during his weekly phone call home. His father reacted angrily, fearing that his son's religion could lead to problems. With hindsight and through reading books abroad that were unavailable to him in China, Changlan understood that his father had suffered during the Cultural Revolution, lost faith in Mao and communism, and was anxious about what would happen to a family with a Christian son, should another period of social turmoil arise. His father's Party membership also complicated matters. Their relationship eased when Changlan returned home and his father observed his normal behavior.

Changlan commented that had he not studied abroad, where he met people with different views of life and the world, he wouldn't have had the opportunity to consider such views. They simply would not have come his way in his home environment.

Return to China: Finding a church

Before Changlan returned to China, his Christian friends found him church contacts in his Chinese city. Then, by going to those churches, he heard about other churches.

Changlan's decision to continue in his new faith, despite his father's initial opposition and a later disagreement when Changlan chose biblical principles over parental help, points to a change in Changlan's values and in his view of where ultimate authority lies.

The biblical narrative that Changlan first heard overseas was reflected in the language he used in our interview. That he also felt he inhabited this ongoing Christian story is reflected in his decision about which church to attend. Every Sunday he and Yin attended a registered church. They referred to other members as their "brothers and sisters." They also participated in a Friday evening marriage group, organized by this church.

Changlan commented on the role members of this church played in keeping him and his then fiancée together during a difficult period. However, his concern that ministers of registered churches are compromised in their ability to preach God's Word led him to attend both this registered church and another, unregistered one, well known for its good teaching and comprehensive Bible coverage:

> It's because in [that] church, and other family churches, the topics are more open. And the message I can get in there is a little bit different from what I can get in the government churches.

Living under the authority of the Bible

The importance Changlan placed on living life in tune with the Bible was underlined by the time he spent reading it, and his familiarity with the contents. This was revealed in his quotation of the Bible in our conversations. He was also helping run a Sunday afternoon Bible study group for returnees.

Changlan's revised view of the world originated abroad, where his prior assumptions were challenged. It developed in a community that shared a common worldview and language (his overseas church) and was sustained and deepened in his church community, and his marriage, after returning to China. His account of life now included a Father God who created the world, is interested in individuals, and has provided a set of standards in the Bible. This affected Changlan's beliefs about marriage. It also led him to see his work and social environment as an opportunity to help others. Authority in his life was no longer vested in his father or in his own strength, but in God.

The importance Changlan attached to following the Bible was evident in his comments about baptism. He didn't get baptized abroad for two reasons: because the Christians he met didn't stress the importance of baptism to him, and because he was concerned about how his father would react if he got baptized. When he returned to China, the church minister was so busy that he didn't ask Changlan if he had been baptized. Only recently had baptism become important to Changlan. In fact, he was planning his baptism when we met. He now saw baptism as having significant meaning and as a command from Christ, and therefore to be obeyed.

Other examples related to relationships. Accounting for the improvement in his relationship with his parents, Changlan mentioned the biblical commandment to honor one's parents. He admitted that his previous tendency to judge his parents, even in light of his perception of their limited thinking and horizons, did not stem from love.

Describing his former sharp tongue and tendency to say things that hurt people, Changlan quoted Psalm 39, saying he now realized his need to "muzzle" his mouth. He mentioned Jesus' comment in Matthew 15:11 that it is what comes out of our mouths that defiles, not what goes in. Even when hurt by colleagues' mockery of his "foreign" beliefs, Changlan resisted the urge to gibe back. He claimed that the habit of muzzling his mouth helped him control his mind.

Fathers and son

When I asked Changlan how he would describe his relationship with God, he spoke of a personal father-son relationship with a God who has a "perfect plan" for his life and who assigns him tasks each day. His conviction that his life has purpose helped him overcome problems and mundanities. His relationship with the Lord varied: sometimes close, sometimes distant. Changlan confessed that sometimes he was "naughty," but God still took care of him.

More than once Changlan referred to the Holy Spirit keeping him out of trouble, reminding him to guard his tongue and giving him strength. He rejected his father's offers to find him a job when he first returned from China and was out of work for some months. It was hard to say no to his father, and it hurt his parents' feelings; but the Spirit convicted him that it was the right thing to do.

Changlan's father wanted him to take a government job, with stability and good benefits. Changlan knew, though, that if he worked for the government he would probably eventually be invited to join the Communist Party. He said, "In just accepting the job, your behavior would have to reflect that there is no God." So even though Changlan knew a government job would bring future perks, such as access to better schooling if he and Yin had a child, he turned his father down. Honoring his earthly father was important, but honoring his eternal Father was more important.

A different view of marriage

Changlan said some striking things about marriage. He met Yin just before they both left to study abroad. They became Christians about the same time and got married four years after returning to China. Changlan was deeply affected by his belief in the existence of God and the authority of the Bible. He described his view that one's marriage partner is sent by God, and therefore marriage should not be treated lightly:

> Divorce is very common in China. My father has six brothers and sisters; two of them divorced already. In relationships in China people tend to think, "It is easy come and easy go" and "Why bother?" Because they do not believe there is a God overhead. They do not believe someone will be getting married with them is the one sent by God. "So who cares? It just happens like (clicks fingers). So it can happen again."

Changlan attributed the continuance of his relationship with his girlfriend, and now wife, to their mutual acceptance of biblical teaching and Christian example. Before he was a Christian, he thought of marriage as a sort of trade with himself at the center:

> I would put myself into the center of this relationship and say, "OK, if you love me, I will love you." And "I deserve to be loved if I love you."

He quoted 1 Corinthians and Ephesians to illustrate his changed view:

> Love is actually a sacrifice, a commitment to each other. "Love is patient, love is kind." So it is really beneficial to our relationship that both of us need to know that. Just like Christ loved the church, you need to sacrifice yourself to each other.

Indeed, being in church, meeting other Christians, helped Changlan develop these ideas during the time he was geographically separated from his then fiancée after returning to China.

Tensions as a new Christian in China

Changlan seemed to be doing well when I met him. He was rooted in his faith, but did experience tensions. When his father first learned he was going to church in England and believed what he heard there, he was angry. He told Changlan, "I didn't want to spend money on you to go to church! I spent money for you to have a better education, not this!"

And despite his initial concerns and consternation when Changlan turned down his help for a government job, five years later his father had come to terms somewhat with Changlan's faith, comforted that his job choice had turned out well. As a manager in a large multinational, he had a decent income and secure prospects.

There was a pervasive belief among family, friends, and wider society that the most important thing was to make money. Going to church was seen as a waste of time, a distraction from more important things.

> Overseas, seems the people would talk about their faith, their life with their family; seems the people there know how to enjoy their life. But in Asia or in China seems people think about how to get more money, or have a better life, etc. I don't call it a "life"; I call it "survival." And people will force you to think that way. They will think, "Oh, it is a luxury to have a faith!"

Work colleagues responded to Changlan's faith in various ways: from interest, to ignoring it as a Western fad, to branding it "crazy." He had learned to hold back his anger when people mocked his beliefs.

At work, Changlan had avoided certain corrupt practices that other returnees have faced—bribery, for example—by determining to work for a well-known multinational. But his colleagues still got involved in heavy after-work drinking sessions, which could lead to other activities that Changlan wanted no part in. Dryly, he commented that being a Christian has benefits. He could avoid these situations by saying, "I'm a Christian; I cannot get drunk. Sorry, it's not my style."

After returning to China, it took Changlan time to adapt to a different church life. He described his experience of the registered church in China:

> You can see in China, it might be because of the cultural difference, people seem to be a little bit distant from each other; they will be very alert to strangers in church. And in terms of the message delivered by the pastor and the churches, I can see there was no limitation in England, but here it seems you can always see the government's involvement, though invisibly. For example, on Christmas Eve you can see the pastors cannot give a very strong gospel message to people, especially outside the church. And even the tract, if they print one, will be inspected by someone who is not in the church. I can see pastors are trying to compromise and negotiate, to do what they can to share the message with the public.

But five years later, although he still sometimes attended services at a famous house church because of the excellent Bible teaching, he viewed the registered church he attended on Sundays and Fridays (for a young-marrieds' group) as his home church. I attended a service there with them;, it was clear that Changlan and Yin were active and well-accepted participants in church life.

New purpose

Before leaving China, Changlan's aims in life centered around being free to explore the world and new ideas, getting a good job (whatever that meant), and being a good son. The man I met was somewhat different. Yes, he still wanted to be a good son, he still enjoys traveling, and he has a good job—indeed, ten years after his return, he has had three good jobs.

Now, though, his relationship with his parents has shifted: He is less concerned about obeying his parents and more concerned about respecting and caring for them. His attitudes toward other people have changed, in marriage and in relationships outside the family: it's less about him being at the center and more about understanding—and being willing to serve—others. He operates in a different social world now: being in church, hearing the Bible taught, spending time with Christian "brothers and sisters" who share his concerns and values. This is all because he has a new idea of the world and himself, which includes needing a good relationship with the God he believes made him.

The Changlan I met sees himself in a Trinitarian Christian narrative, as a sinner, saved by Christ, helped by the Holy Spirit, with a new future, under the control of God the Father:

> In terms of commitment to Christ, I would say now I can see my life has a purpose; so whenever I face difficulties, or unexpected changes in my life, I'm not afraid. And I won't be disappointed by the challenges I would face tomorrow or in the future because I believe that God has a perfect plan in my life, even though sometimes I may be in the depths and sometimes I may be in the peaks. And I can see my mind will not be easily influenced by society because there's always the Holy Spirit reminding us what is right and wrong.

Ling: "I Felt Like a Thief"

Ling was twenty-six, single, and had been back in China three years when we met. She left China at age twenty-two and spent a year doing a master's degree in engineering.

"Study, study": The early years

In her earliest years, Ling lived with her grandparents; her parents took her home once a week. She was their only child. Her grandmother was a primary school teacher and they lived in a flat at the school; Ling enjoyed playing with the other children.

At six, Ling went to live with her parents and started school. Her father had a university degree and worked as an engineer; her mother had a high school education and worked in the textile industry. Ling described her school years as being "study, study." Middle school was particularly hard, with strict, unhelpful teachers:

> I had lots of homework. That's a very, very, very heavy load for me. I didn't like that time.

Relief came in the form of relationships with cousins and friends, although school vacations were lonely times. Trips to other cities with her grandparents, and her father's interest for Canada, gave Ling the idea of one day studying abroad.

Religion? "Maybe there is something"

As a child, Ling didn't believe in the supernatural. Her grandparents believed in ghosts and celebrated the Qingming festival.

> We would bring food to the tomb, to see the dead, and sometimes we would have a meal at home and get the meal ready and . . . we can't eat at that time. We would say, "Let them (the dead) eat first," and after a while we started.

Ling's mother, who was a member of the Communist Party, told her that the supernatural "doesn't exist"; and Ling herself didn't believe in it because she could see that the food remained uneaten and was eventually eaten by the family.

At university, Ling had a boyfriend whose parents were Catholics, but he never went to church. Ling never thought deeply about religion and never met Christians until she went overseas. Later, in her baptism testimony, she wrote:

> I did believe that there must be some kind of "God" but I did not know who he was. And as there are so many stories told by elderly people, I believed a little bit in Buddhism. However, I did believe that this world must be controlled by a certain god. There is a Chinese story which is similar to the Genesis description of creation, and the ancient people in China had similar opinions about how the earth was created.

Ling went to a temple near her undergraduate university a few times, somehow attracted to it. She commented, "At that time I began to realize maybe there is something in the world we can't see, but I don't know what it is. So I went to the temple and kind of prayed."

Smooth relationships

At eighteen Ling went to study environmental engineering at a university two hours from her home. She hoped to do something to combat the environmental problems that young people were becoming aware of; she remembered being touched by Michael Jackson's song "Heal the World," which was popular then. She was a little disappointed when she found out her program was more about mechanics and equipment than telling people how to save the planet!

Nevertheless, Ling's university days were good. She enjoyed the independence from her parents, although she was near enough that they expected her to go home once a month. She liked managing her own affairs and particularly enjoyed the way she and her classmates looked after each other—for example, if one of them was ill.

Good relationships with friends were particularly important. To my surprise, when I asked Ling about the highlight of her undergraduate time, she mentioned the 2003 SARS (severe acute respiratory syndrome) epidemic. Classes stopped and students weren't permitted to leave campus. Sporting activities were organized to strengthen the students against the disease. Ling enjoyed the closer friendships that arose from the enforced enclosure.

Her saddest memory of university also related to a friendship—with her roommate. They became less close when Ling started spending time with a boyfriend. Before, they had talked about everything, shared everything. But then, Ling said, "She didn't tell me her real thoughts and maybe I didn't tell her mine either."

Enjoying a peaceful life

Ling's father wanted her to study abroad. Eager to travel, Ling gladly applied—and was accepted—to a master's program in the UK. At a reception in China that the university held for new students about to travel to the UK, Ling met someone who was to become a close friend. Ling and Sky clicked immediately, and supported each other throughout the next year.

Ling also enjoyed the friendship of other Chinese students; they encouraged each other, cooking together and providing academic support in the radically different university context. Ling appreciated the quieter, peaceful UK life and the beautiful university campus. She made the most of opportunities to visit historic cities and see the countryside.

Life was generally pleasant, except Ling, like many Chinese students, was uneasy going out at night. In China, there were always a lot of people around the shops at night. In the UK, the empty, dark streets were intimidating. The only really anxious time, though, was when the university informed Ling's father that she had failed an exam. She had planned to take the exam again and pass without him knowing.

Assumptions challenged

When a Chinese Malaysian friend invited Ling to a Bible study and some other Christian events, Ling initially turned him down. She was wary, not knowing what it was all about. However, when she and Sky later accepted his invitation to a campus meeting of international Christian students, they were impressed by the kindness and openness they encountered:

> You know, they are always smiling, and they are nice. They always help other people. I thought, "If that's a Christian, I like them."

This was Ling's first encounter with Christians. She was surprised that most people there were ethnically Chinese. This challenged her previously unquestioned assumption that Christianity and being Chinese didn't go together.

> I never imagined I would meet a Christian like him, because he is Chinese Malaysian. His grandparents are Chinese, and his parents are Chinese. Just their nationality is Malaysian. I didn't know that, because everyone around me . . . all didn't believe any religious thing, or they believed in Buddha. So I thought it [Christianity] was very far from me.

After this positive experience, when they heard that Chinese New Year was to be celebrated at the international café held every week in a church near campus, Ling and Sky felt confident enough to give it a try. From then on, this was a weekly highlight. She enjoyed these people's company and became curious to find out what they believed. Her English and Chinese Christian friends had a different worldview and understanding of life, including things she had previously thought untrue.

After attending a weekly introduction to Christianity course, attending church, reading books, and questioning friends, Ling eventually decided that what she was discovering in the Bible, including the resurrection of Jesus, was true—and decided to become a Christian. She remembered a special moment when a mainland Chinese Christian friend prayed for her. Ling felt convinced then that Christianity was true and was touched to tears.

Ling was baptized three months before she returned to China. Her written baptism testimony includes a description of God as Father and of our sins being "washed out through the death of Jesus because of our faith." She also wrote:

> It is wonderful to think that God is with us, always, though I am not used to it now. I think I will soon get used to it through God's guide and other friends' help.

This may indicate there was a slight doubt in Ling's mind at that point. Certainly the lack of Christian friends around her proved difficult later, when she returned to China.

After her baptism Ling successfully completed her master's thesis. She continued to attend a local church on Sundays and also joined a weekly English-speaking fellowship of young people from British-born and Hong Kong backgrounds. She met very few mainland Chinese Christians. Her preparation specifically for the mainland consisted of one conversation about church with a mainland Chinese Christian.

Ling had a fixed-date return ticket to China. As the September date drew near, she faced a dilemma: should she throw away the ticket and look for a job abroad or return to China and seek a job during the best season for job-hunting? China offered better job prospects, but she was concerned about the church in China and didn't want to leave her UK church and Christian friends. The decision was essentially made for her when she was invited to a job interview in her home city in China.

Return home: Church tensions

Ling's job interview was successful. The search for a church was more difficult. A Christian overseas had advised her, perhaps unfortunately, against going to a registered church in case they toed the Communist Party line too much. But she had concerns about unregistered churches too.

> The difficult thing was church: looking for a good church, and to tell which church is good, which church is bad, and to look for groups. They were aware of me, they were very careful, because they didn't know who I am and they didn't know if I am a real Christian or just a fake one. I was very careful too. I wasn't sure if it was Jehovah's Witnesses or things like that.

After some months, Ling found an unregistered church where she was made welcome and the Bible was faithfully taught, but it was very different than what she had experienced overseas. There was no local minister and the preachers traveled from another city each Sunday. And there were no midweek home groups. For these two reasons the church met all day Sunday, with preaching first and then fellowship. After a hard week at work, Ling found this exhausting.

Ling was also uncomfortable with the church's need to hide:

> They rent a flat; they move maybe half a year later, moving from here to there. They don't want to be discovered. I don't understand that because I think, "We're Christians and it's really not a thing to be ashamed of, but we are doing things . . . like we are thieves. We can't let other people know what we are doing here." I don't like the feeling. You know, in England everybody says "I'm a Christian" so proudly. I like that.

Parents and marriage prospects

Attending church also triggered conflict with Ling's parents. They objected to her spending so much time at church and wanted her to spend more time with them. They were also eager for her to marry and somewhat frustrated when she expressed a desire to marry only a Christian.

For the first year, Ling was certain she would only marry a Christian. However, as she became twenty-four, then twenty-five, her parents were arranging dates for her and she felt people were looking at her and wondering why she was still single. Since Ling herself wanted to get married and have a family, it became more and more of a struggle to turn away from someone purely because he wasn't a Christian. She became less certain:

> Sometimes when parents give you pressure and someone is good to you . . . it's really hard.

By the time we met, Ling had stopped going to church. A year later she married a man who was not a Christian, and with whom she is very happy. They have a young son.

Peer pressure

When Ling returned to China, she quietly let some friends and colleagues know that she had become a Christian. She was puzzled that they found her decision odd; she felt a critical edge to their curiosity.

Initially Ling tried to "stick by the rules." Her peers consulted horoscopes and liked watching horror movies and going drinking together. She felt that a good Christian shouldn't be involved in these things, but gradually she found that she could bear to be with these friends. At first when Ling was asked, "What is your horoscope animal?" she would say, "I don't believe in that." But eventually she started to tell them which animal. She continued to avoid certain films, and when they were discussed she would just listen without joining in.

A blessing: A new perspective on money and striving

However, Ling experienced a change that was a real blessing to her and which her friends thought might be good, albeit rather strange: she had become generous. Her comments suggested that since her time abroad, Ling put a high value on being generous and on being content with what she had rather than striving for more money and possessions. She told me her life was easier than others' because she didn't worry about money or achieving higher position. People had commented that she had changed since going abroad.

> They say I seem to be paying less attention to money. Everybody was hoping to get more money, or to be rich overnight, and I just don't care about that too much.

Ling said that before studying abroad her aim in life was to get a good job, make plenty of money, and buy her father a Mercedes-Benz. Now she laughed at her former self. She linked this change with being a Christian and connecting with Christians overseas. She had been impressed by their generosity and willingness to take people out or give them rides. They would pay for international students' meals when they were out together and donate money to the church, all without expecting something back for their investment. These Christians were not stingy, not "iron roosters." In China, a proverbial iron rooster (铁公鸡 or *tiěgōngjī*) won't give up even one of its feathers. Its feathers are so hard to pluck out that it may as well be made of iron.

Changed or not?

Ling claimed to have changed during her year abroad. Rather than money, she now wanted "a peaceful, joyful life, and to be happy with all the friends and relatives." Her sense of contentment and lack of desire for money and status was at odds with the values of many around her. She attributed this to seeing a more relaxed way of life overseas *and* to being a Christian:

> The living style the British people are having, I think is very good. They are having, compared to us, a slower life. And they looked happier. And they are very polite to other people; and I think they are polite from their hearts, not just showing to other people "I'm a polite person."

> I think the simple life, when you are reaching to God and you pay less attention to material things, you can be happier.

Ling also said:

> I changed in the UK, and I remained when I came back; but I changed a bit back to the person I was before.

Looking back to the time before she decided to believe, Ling said she had been afraid that if she found she could not believe she would hate, or disrespect, Christians. It had been, and remained, extremely important to her to maintain harmonious, respectful relationships and to fit in with others.

When I asked Ling about the biggest change in her life, she replied, "Of course, becoming a Christian." Now that she is married, has a young child, and is no longer part of a Christian community, I wonder if she would give the same answer. After Ling returned to China, the Christian story and self-concept she identified with overseas was not consolidated within a Christian church community. Her interviews were full of references to Christian friends in the UK. When I asked Ling to define her relationship with God, she described him as an invisible father and very good friend; but references to an active God, common in other interviews, were few in hers.

Ling's church experience after her return, the critical reaction of others to her being a Christian, the idea that she should marry only a Christian, and her parents' objections all combined to draw her away from church. It's hard to know whether Christ was part of Ling's continued daily thinking or the context of the interview led to her say that becoming a Christian represented the biggest change in her life; she may have wanted not to disturb our friendly relationship.

She said:

> When I first came back, the change was obvious. But now it's . . . I think I'm affected by other people.

Although Ling said she differed from others in having less desire for money and status, without continued Christian friendships and church involvement, her self-concept may not have changed much from before she went abroad. Ling still wanted to be a good daughter, have a happy, peaceful family life, and get along well with those around her. Her ideas were certainly challenged when she went abroad and met Christians, but it's hard to say whether deep, sustained change has happened. Her strongest value (being in a warm, mutually supportive community and having unruffled, respectful relationships with those closest to her) remained unchanged.

For some interviewees being part of an overseas Christian community represented a step toward a radically changed master story, self-concept, and values that continued in a Christian community after returning to China. For Ling that seemed not to be the case. Perhaps it was the happy community rather than the Christian gospel that she "believed in." Or perhaps she understood and accepted the gospel, was born again, and struggled when transplanted to a different soil in China—but is still in the care of the great Father God who yet has plans for her. Do pray.

Luli: No Longer Seeking a Million-yuan Man

The years before Luli left China to study for a master's degree were years of struggle and searching: searching for a man who would make her financially secure, even wealthy. She didn't find this kind of wealth or love overseas, but she did experience a crisis that led her to God.

Early life: Family and money struggles

Luli was born in Central China in 1976, the youngest of three siblings. Her early life was hard. Initially her family wasn't that poor. Her father was respected in the village for his knowledge and ability. Despite his education ending because of the Cultural Revolution, he had some training in a technical school, and worked for a while in a school. Luli's mother only had a primary education.

Unfortunately, Luli's parents argued constantly, causing her nightmares. When she was still small, the family moved to a town where her father was involved in setting up a factory. However, he went away a lot, eventually lost his job, and gradually returned home less and less. Although Luli's mother worked in the factory, they had very little to live on. Lack of money intensified the arguments between Luli's parents.

Luli's relationship with her mother was a great strain on her during her teen years. She felt ashamed of their poverty and grew determined to do something about it. When Luli was in high school, the teacher would repeatedly ask her to pay her fees. Luli was intensely ashamed that she couldn't do so, and feared her classmates finding out.

When I asked Luli if she had any specific hope or ambition as a teenager, she replied,

> I think I had one wish. I just wanted to stop my mum complaining. I thought money could satisfy her, because she complained about the money thing. So I wanted to be independent; I wanted to make money. I wanted to give her money so she cannot complain about my father.

Despite being an excellent student, Luli failed the all-important university entrance exam. Her desperation to get to university, her teacher's high expectations of her, and her father's absence all made her so stressed that she ended up being too ill to take the two-day exam. A year later, she retook the exam and obtained a good enough score to embark on a university course to become an English teacher. Luli chose this program for financial reasons: she qualified for a scholarship toward fees and living expenses, and the prospects of finding a job in this field were good.

Although finances were still a worry, Luli's mother managed to give her some money to start the program, and Luli found a part-time teaching job. She worked hard. She was driven to succeed academically, get a good job, and gain sufficient financial independence. She wanted to end her mother's ceaseless complaints about money. In her final year Luli briefly had a boyfriend, a kind young man who did teaching practice in the same school. After graduation, however, Yimu moved to Shanghai to work. They didn't know it then, but their paths would cross again later.

After graduation: Looking for love and money

Money pressures continued after graduation. Luli's older brother started university and needed financial support, and she wanted to save to buy her mother a flat. For so long the family had gone from rented place to rented place, moving on when they became unable to pay. Luli realized that her teacher's salary wouldn't be enough for all this. With help from a pupil's father, she got a job in a trading company—taking on private students to supplement her income.

Looking for a husband who could provide for her financially, Luli started dating a man.

> I talked to that guy: "When you've got one million yuan we can get married." That's what I said. Now I think it was really ridiculous.

Luli knew he loved her, but she didn't really love him. After his company moved him to another city, with better prospects, he phoned to tell her he was near the one million and asked her to join him. In the meantime, however, Luli had fallen for someone else. She left her job and moved to Beijing to join this new boyfriend, who helped her financially. For a while she didn't even need to work, and she followed him when he moved south to set up a business. When the business failed, their relationship broke down and her boyfriend asked her to leave.

Talking to me, Luli reflected that she had been very selfish, not concerned about what her boyfriend was going through. Eventually she returned to her home city, moving in with her brother and his family.

However, before Luli moved back home she stayed with Jing, an old university friend who was now married. She knew these friends had become Christians and she saw that they had a happy, peaceful marriage. Luli had no previous knowledge of Christianity, apart from the idea that Christians were nice people, gained from meeting two foreigners studying at her university. Now Jing told her about Jesus and the Bible.

Although Luli remembered that this encouraged her during her depression, she couldn't "fully understand or accept it." She didn't feel there really was a God. She thought this was just something for weak people to rely on, and she didn't want to be a weak person.

Luli started planning to study abroad in order to become qualified for a higher position. She also dreamed of leaving China because she thought living conditions would be better abroad, and because "the relationship between people is not so complicated as in China."

She was back with her former boyfriend. The plan was that he would support Luli through her master's year abroad. But when he lost money on investments, he tried to break up and said he couldn't support her study. Luli pleaded with him desperately: "Have you ever thought of me? I'm a thirty-year-old woman. What can I do?" He gave in, saying he would try to support her, even though he wasn't sure how.

With a belief in her boyfriend's ability to make money and the idea that, once she had settled in the UK, he would join her and easily get a good job, Luli flew off to start her master's program.

Overseas: God's voice in the crisis

At the same time, however, something else was happening. A month before Luli left, she learned that her dear brother had liver cancer. He was only thirty-two, and had a wife and small child. "All of us felt desperate," Luli recalled. "Each time I saw him I could not stop crying."

Luli knew that her brother had become a Christian. His Christian university teachers and colleagues, and even some church teachers from Hong Kong, came to visit him.

> I witnessed a lot in hospital. So I was touched really. I just felt the love between the Christians. I thought, "This is really a good thing, even though I don't know whether there is really a God or not."

Luli also saw how strong her brother was emotionally. He insisted she carry on with her plan to go abroad and asked her to go to church there. So when Luli arrived, she kept her eyes open for a church.

> Actually, what church is, I didn't know, or what church people do. I just wanted to find the church and they are good people. I would feel safer there.

During her first week, Luli met some people advertising opportunities to study the Bible. They had material in Chinese too. These people came to Luli's place once a week for about three months. However, Luli felt that they weren't like the Christians she had met with her brother in China.

> They didn't say the love thing; they didn't say "Jesus Christ"; they didn't say the family thing, you know.

Luli felt that something was wrong even though she wasn't equipped to judge.

Then, at Christmas, Luli got the devastating news that her boyfriend had broken off the relationship. This also meant she had no way of paying for her university fees and housing. After crying alone in her room for two days, she contacted her old friend Jing in China. Jing told her this was the time to think about the real source and meaning of her life. She explained more about the love of God and the purpose of Christ's death on the cross. She also helped Luli identify that the people she had been studying the Bible with were Jehovah's Witnesses.

Over MSN, Jing led Luli in a prayer of commitment to Christ. She insisted Luli stop meeting with the Jehovah's Witnesses and prayed she would meet Christians. Then Luli talked to a Taiwanese classmate she had seen reading the Bible. The classmate introduced Luli to a Christian university chaplain, who then introduced her to a local church with a Chinese-speaking fellowship. A church member gave her a room, rent-free.

Luli remarked that in the midst of this crisis she believed God was calling her to him, giving her a "second chance." This reminded me of words written by C. S. Lewis: "God whispers to us in our pleasures, speaks to us in our conscience, but shouts in our pains: it is His *megaphone* to rouse a *deaf* world."[73] Just as for Fuyin and three other women I interviewed, Luli's crisis induced a sense of helplessness and a belief that her own ability was insufficient to cope. With this came a new openness to God.

Throughout the roller coaster that was the rest of her time overseas, Luli was guarded in Christ by the peace of God. Despite the generosity of her new friends and her own hard work in part-time jobs, her financial problems didn't disappear. Her brother's health deteriorated, and her concern about him was increased by the miles between them. She thought about going home to look after him, but he insisted that she complete her program.

One day Luli was full of joy after hearing that her mother had started to believe; the next day she was mugged in the street outside her house. Fearing she wouldn't see her brother again, she flew back to China, only to arrive a few hours after he died.

Despite all this, Luli could look back at this period and say,

> I think the life there was the happiest time I had in my whole life. I think belief is the center. Without belief I think I could not survive there really, without God. The most encouraging is God's words from the Bible. Actually, I had quite a lot of debts, but I really didn't worry about it. The life, the friendship, and the fellowship: it was a really good time for me.

Luli could see that God was taking care of her and also that he was changing her parents. Although she was very sad about losing her brother, she could cope because her brother was a Christian and because she trusted God.

Following Christ in the workplace

In the UK, Luli attended church regularly and was also a committed member of a Mandarin-speaking home fellowship. She read her Bible avidly and listened to sermons again online to ensure she understood them. She started to care for others and to think how her gifts and career could serve God; and her understanding of the purpose and potential nature of marriage was turned on its head.

Luli's reading of the Bible and conversation with Christian friends led her to pray that she would be a good steward of the qualification, abilities, and experience she had been given. With her visa running out and little chance of a job, she returned to China, moving straight to Shanghai to look for a job.

A Taiwanese friend emailed Luli an ad about a job in Shanghai. She not only got the job but worked for that small HR consultancy for eight years. Luli wasn't highly paid, but as a consultant to other companies she contributed

---

73   C. S. Lewis, *The Problem of Pain* (London: Fount, 1977 [1940]), 74.

to improving conditions for workers. She could have earned more and thus afforded a nicer apartment in a different job, but she chose to stay because her work made a positive difference in others' lives and her bosses had high moral standards. Working for them didn't involve her in unethical business practices. The job with the highest salary was no longer her goal. (Years later, when her husband's health forced him to leave his job, Luli moved to a better-paid job but they continued to live simply.)

Marriage and church life in China

Soon after her return to China, Luli met up with Yimu, her kind boyfriend in the final year of undergraduate study. She shared the gospel with him, and he believed. Soon afterward he asked her to marry him, and Luli didn't hesitate. He might not be rich, but she knew he was trustworthy and she could love him. Luli's mother objected because Yimu didn't have much money; but after praying, Luli made her own decision.

Settling in a church was harder. When I met Luli she was going to a registered church. It was quite formal, and there were over a thousand people at the service I attended with her. She didn't know anyone there; people rushed out as soon as the last hymn started. The one advantage was that the church was within walking distance of the small flat Luli and Yimu had recently moved to in order to be nearer her work. This was important because Luli was pregnant with their first child.

Prior to this Luli and Yimu had been in two house churches. They even tried holding a fellowship group for young married couples in their home, but it lacked support. They commented that the church had fellowship groups for the church workers but wasn't good at helping ordinary members. Luli missed the close friendship and fellowship she had experienced in the UK. Being pregnant made it harder, since she was so tired.

Living with mother-in-law

Luli was struggling to get along with her parents, who had lived apart for many years. Her mother still complained to her over the phone about her father. Luli said that because she had never had a close relationship with her own mother she was struggling in her relationship with her husband's mother, who had recently arrived in Shanghai to live with them and help with the new baby. At that time the family was living in a tiny two-room flat, sharing kitchen facilities with other families.

Luli's mother-in-law chose to believe in Christ not long after she moved to Shanghai. Luli said her mother-in-law was reaching out to her, wanting to be close, but she didn't know how to respond.

> I think it's a chance to learn things. But for now I don't really feel that I can do it, that I can get this right, because—first of all—I didn't get along with my own mother.

Pregnancy, a demanding job, the arrival of Yimu's mother to live in their tiny apartment, lack of close Christian fellowship—these were all piling up to make Luli very weary when I met her. Fortunately, this has changed in the years since, and even then Luli spoke glowingly about how God was at work in her marriage.

A Christian marriage

Yimu's upbringing had been heavily influenced by Buddhism. In the early months of his faith and their marriage, his ideas were somewhat confused. Luli grew anxious when he misinterpreted Christian and biblical concepts in the light of Buddhism.

> We quarreled a bit about his beliefs. He just mixed them up; I couldn't bear it.

Luli kept praying for Yimu privately. He read the Bible more and more, and meeting other Christians from a similar background helped him understand the difference between Christianity and Buddhism.

Both Luli and Yimu told me, independently, that if God had not intervened, their marriage would not have survived. They argued during the first six months they were married, Luli sometimes reverting to her old impetuous self. But Yimu's understanding and faith were growing, and they were increasingly able to talk and help each other. A church "sister" helped by talking things through with them. Luli told me that if she had still been the old self-centered, impatient person that she was before following Christ, the arguments would have led to divorce. Without me even raising the issue, Yimu told me he couldn't imagine the hot-tempered Luli of university days staying; she would have walked out of the marriage.

Luli's ideas of marriage had been transformed since she believed in Christ and sought to follow biblical teaching. When I asked her in what ways she had changed, she answered:

> Now I just think the money that I can make a living, just to live a normal life, that will be OK for me. I will not want to make more money for a better life. You know, that's not what I'm pursuing now. I wanted to find a person who is wealthy, is supportive of me. But now I've changed that. I've changed my mind. I just want to find a person who is responsible, who is caring, and just a quite equal relationship.

She attributed the changes in her attitudes to money and to marriage to different causes:

> The money thing . . . I think it is my experience. My past experiences just made me understand that money cannot solve all problems. So I think this is one reason. But the marriage thing, the relationship thing, I think God changed me; because the Bible teaches me what a relationship with God is like. And also the relationship between husband and wife is not like what I believed before. It should be the husband is the head, and the wife should be submitted to her husband. I'd never thought of it. Before, I thought, "I am the center. He should take care of all my feelings, my concerns." So that's totally different now. I need to support my husband. I need to consider his feelings, his problems. So that is what God teaches me.

Knowing other Christian couples also helped. At first Luli didn't know how to apply what she read in the Bible to her own marriage; but her married sisters and brothers gave suggestions on "how to do the right thing in God's eyes."

So what has changed?

I have visited Luli and her family several times since I interviewed her. Luli and Yimu, their two children, and both of Yimu's parents now all live together. They own their flat and, although it is small, the atmosphere is happy and welcoming.

They talk about how God has been good to them, not least in providing their current church, a house church that they moved to some years ago. They have settled well there. Yimu leads a small group. They both describe this church in warm terms; the Bible teaching is good, there is provision for children, and church friends were prayerful and supportive during Yimu's illness. They even moved to a ground-floor apartment, which they specially adapted to make it easier to have small group meetings in their home: an extra door enables people to enter the flat without disturbing neighbors who might report the meetings.

Being guided by God and being in fellowship with other Christians (in marriage and in church) is crucial for Luli. She is sustained in her faith and life by sharing with Christians who, like her, put strong emphasis on love, prayer, and following God's written Word.

Before meeting God overseas, Luli's whole life was desperately focused on finding a man to love her and lift her family out of their financial difficulties and troubled relationships. Impressed by the peace and love shown by Christians, she committed to trusting God in the midst of a crisis. Now she sees herself as rescued by God to a security greater than money. She trusts God for her family's future too. Before, she felt trapped and in danger of destitution. Now she can laugh, love, and enjoy serving others—inside and outside her family. She wants them to know the God she knows, who loves her and has set her free.

Comparing her life as a Christian with her life before, Luli said:

> This is just a totally different life I'm living; because without God, I would have a different life. I can't imagine sometimes. I would just be messy or struggling. I don't think I would have a good life without God's work on me, or his help.

Jinjing: Christianity?
Someone Else's Story

Jinjing was forty-two when she arrived in the UK for a year as a visiting scholar. Her husband visited her there briefly, but didn't have the sustained contact with Christians and the church that she did. Three years after she returned to her job teaching English at a university in a northern provincial capital, I met Jinjing in her home.

In the UK, Jinjing made some kind of profession of faith, but back in China she told me she was "confused" about God and had not been meeting with Christians. First, let's trace the story she told me about her life, then what her time abroad meant to her, particularly her view of the Bible.

A loving home

Jinjing described a happy childhood; she was the youngest of six siblings and much loved by her parents. Her father was already fifty when Jinjing was born and had died many years earlier. As an adult, Jinjing learned that her father went to a Christian school. Little Jinjing loved sitting next to him in the yard at night, listening to his stories. Years later, in the UK, she realized that many of the stories her father told her were from the Bible. She guessed that he hadn't mentioned that because this was during the Cultural Revolution (1966 to 1976), when it would have been dangerous to do so.

Jinjing described her father as uncommonly kind, attentive, and patient. When I asked if she thought he might have been a Christian but couldn't say so, she said, "Yes, maybe." Religion wasn't discussed in the home, and young Jinjing had no conscious encounter with religion or interest in it.

Determination for education

Because Jinjing's parents supported her desire to go to university, they sent her to a weekly boarding school. She was one of only two students from her village. However, at this point universities had only just reopened after being closed during the Cultural Revolution; a change in entrance requirements meant Jinjing failed in her first attempt to get in. Also, spots went first to older adults who had been unable to go while the universities were closed.

So, at eighteen, Jinjing went to a technical college to study English from scratch. It wasn't until she had been a school teacher for three years that she eventually went to university, studying in the evenings while continuing to teach during the day. Life was hard, but good.

Romance, marriage, and career

When Jinjing was twenty-six, her older sister introduced her to the man who would become her husband. Her sister thought it was time Jinjing married. Jinjing laughed at the memory. As a young woman, she loved reading foreign novels: *Gone with the Wind*, *Wuthering Heights*, *Anna Karenina*, Jane Austen's books. When her suitor told her that he was an army journalist, she thought, "Oh, someone creative; how romantic . . . like Hemingway!" Although her husband wasn't quite the romantic figure Jinjing originally imagined, their marriage has been a happy one. When we met, their eighteen-year-old son was preparing to study abroad.

After teaching in schools for several years, Jinjing decided that teaching in a university would offer more security. She earned a master's degree by studying part time, and then received a university post. However, Jinjing still felt her English was inadequate, so she jumped at the chance, in 2005, to go abroad as a visiting scholar. She could improve her English and fulfill a dream of seeing what English people's lives were really like.

UK: Exploring culture

Jinjing's experience in the UK was mixed. It met her expectations in regard to opportunities to visit places related to her literary interests and to learn about English culture. Another Chinese scholar introduced her to a weekly social activity: a café for international students at a church near the university. There Jinjing met people willing to answer her many questions, particularly a well-informed retired man who took her and some friends to visit historic sites.

The people Jinjing met at the café also supported her when she needed hospital treatment and after an intruder broke into the house she rented. Because she was drawn to the Christians, Jinjing went to a Bible-overview course for international students and attended church regularly.

However, before Jinjing met Christians, she met Jehovah's Witnesses. On just her third day in the UK, she met another visiting scholar who had been invited by a "Christian" to attend church but didn't want to go alone. So the two went together and were then invited to the Witnesses' home. They enjoyed cooking together. The people were kind, and a time was arranged for the Witnesses to visit them to study the Bible. But here's how Jinjing compared her experiences with the Jehovah's Witnesses and the international café:

> We met the people at the café. I thought it was quite different from the Jehovah's Witnesses. It made us very happy. I talked with my friend [about the Jehovah's Witnesses] and said, "This is something like the Cultural Revolution in China: 'You can't do this, can't do that.'" And they asked very simple questions, according to their magazine—not the Bible.

Initially Jinjing and her friend simply avoided the Witnesses, not wanting to turn down people who had helped them. Eventually, though, they told them they didn't want to meet with them and focussed instead on the Christian café and church.

God and the Bible: For the Chinese too?

Throughout our conversations, Jinjing talked about the Bible, and God to a degree, but not about Jesus, sin, or salvation. When I prompted her to share about what she believed when she was in England, she described how that differed from what she thought now, back in China.

Before going abroad, Jinjing had thought that God was for the Jews and for some people in other countries, but not for the Chinese. She had viewed Jesus like someone from a fable. When Jinjing met Christians abroad and studied the Bible with them, she started to question her assumptions. She and another Chinese scholar discussed these things and came to the conclusion that there had to be a ruler God. There was no other explanation for the world; someone must be in control.

A church worker showed Jinjing where the Bible says that God cares for the whole world. She explained that what the Bible says is for people of all countries, including China. At the time this seemed reasonable, and Jinjing was very happy to hear it. She changed her mind about Jesus too, deciding that he was a real person. However, as I spoke with Jinjing in China, although it was clear that she believed in the existence of God and Jesus, I heard no evidence that she had any concept of herself as a sinner or of Jesus as a savior.

> To tell you the truth, when I got back home, the surroundings changed, the environment changed, so I did not think so much about Jesus and church.

Back in China: Away from Christians, away from God?

Before leaving the UK, Jinjing attended a Christian workshop to help prepare returnees to return to their countries. She was given a workbook entitled *Think Home*, which she used for a little while after returning to China. Jinjing never went to a church; she said she was too busy with work or doing something with her husband. And it would have taken four hours of her time because the only church she knew of was on the other side of the city. Jinjing didn't read the Bible or pray regularly. When I asked if she considered herself a Christian, she said,

> I think I tried to be a real Christian, but I don't think I am, because I don't think I do what God asks us to do. And I'm not doing the best, I think, because I never go to church and I only seldom read the Bible. Sometimes I was confused and I can't understand things in the Bible, so I just wonder.

After returning to China, Jinjing said that sometimes she believed in God, but other times she was "in chaos, confused." She sometimes thought, "Where is God? Does God know me? Can he hear me?" God seemed relevant for the UK context, but not for China. She reverted to the idea that God was probably only for some nationalities, but not for the Chinese. In the UK, Jinjing had seen a peaceful, loving, churchgoing way of life that she wanted for herself; but she hadn't understood the real good news of the gospel or her need for it.

When I asked Jinjing if she felt her motivations in life had changed, she was puzzled—reflecting that she had never considered what her motivations were.

The Book about love

Despite all this, God may be using Jinjing to encourage others to read the Bible. She revered the Bible as "the book of love"; this came from what she read of it in the UK and from observing the lives of Christians there. Jinjing was also deeply impressed by a Christian professor at her UK university who incorporated the Bible's teaching about love into his teaching methods and research.

Jinjing's experience abroad led her to develop in her undergraduate teaching in China a new module regarding how the Bible has affected Western culture.

> I think this is a great fruit of when I was in the UK, and I hope never to forget this experience. I think the Bible really influenced people's life values—even the society, politics, culture, music, and architecture. So I want to introduce more to my students, to the people around me. Maybe if they think my course is attractive, maybe they will believe in the Bible. They will understand more and change their life. This is my wish. Now I think maybe one of the main ideas or themes of the Bible, or what I learned in church, is love. If all the people loved each other, just like sisters and brothers, there would be no war, and no terrible things happening in the world. The world would be peaceful. I think it is a good thing; it's good for everyone.

Jinjing has also followed her UK friends' example by inviting international students in her university to her home to show them love and to introduce them to her culture.

Resisting the drive for more

> After returning to China, Jinjing became concerned about the pervasive culture of striving for more. She noticed that British people had peaceful lives and time to think, whereas the Chinese struggled so much. They had worked so hard to insure against future hard times that now they couldn't stop wanting more and more—a better car or apartment than their neighbor, more money, or more power.

Jinjing thought this led to conflict between people, and the best response was to "just worship God, do your own work well, help each other, try your best to make the harmonious environment." She could see this desperate striving in her husband—likening him to the *Gone with the Wind* character Scarlett O'Hara, who had fought her way out of poverty but could never be satisfied with what she had, even when she was well-off.

Recently a close friend and colleague had died. He was only Jinjing's age. She believed he was killed by the stress of working too hard, doing a PhD while still working full time. Because of this, Jinjing was resisting the pressure to get a PhD in order to progress in her career. She shared about an idea for after her retirement: starting something a bit like church, with Bible study and people caring for each other. Perhaps this was more of a dream, rekindled by my questions, than a plan.

In addition to accepting her material situation, Jinjing said she accepted other people more easily because of her time abroad:

I think I can understand others better than before. Because God said we are ordinary people, we have no right to judge others; that means who is right and who is wrong. So I think only God has the right to do that. So I just do what I want to do. I never complain about other people's motives.

Jinjing mentioned an old school friend who has been a Christian a long time but lives on the other side of China. Before studying abroad, Jinjing sometimes talked to her about quarrels with her husband or something else on her mind; the friend advised her to listen to God and "not to care about trifles." Jinjing said she now tries to do that.

Someone else's story

I came away from my conversations with Jinjing with a strong sense that she looked at Christians' lives as having something very good, which attracted her, but as being separate from her—not *her* story. She referred wistfully to their peaceful lives. She looked at her UK professor, saw how famous he was, how many books he had written, yet he seemed not to be stressed. She commented that he saw his work as doing something for God, so this helped him relax.

I found his teaching method is full of love. This love, I think, comes from God, the Bible. So his class environment is harmonious, and his attitude to his job and to the students is quite, quite special. I think his work . . . that means his book, is full of the spirit of love. I think these ideas, all this theme, maybe comes from . . . how to say . . . it's because he is a Christian.

Missing: The experience of Christianity as Chinese

Jinjing seemed to perceive her experience with Christianity as cultural. She viewed her overseas experience of Christian activities as related, yes, to the Bible, but also to British culture. Because she had not perceived Christianity as something separate from Britain, that also existed in China, she never sought out a church upon her return. Jinjing didn't have the Chinese Christian sense of belonging in God's family that other interviewees had; and she had not understood Christ's significance.

Many of the participants in my research had contact with Chinese Christians while abroad. Some attended Chinese churches. Some attended local English-speaking churches and also participated in a Mandarin-speaking fellowship. Some simply had a Chinese Christian friend.

Jinjing's situation was different. She attended an English-speaking church with strong Bible teaching, opportunities for international students to study the Bible, and people who cared for her. But she wasn't exposed to Chinese Christians worshiping God and following him, and she had no Chinese Christian friend to talk to in Chinese. So even though Jinjing gave verbal assent to the biblical proposition that God was calling people from all nations, including China, she never really felt it. The idea never settled in her imagination. Perhaps the mental picture of Christianity being *Chinese* never really entered her subconscious.

What changed; What did not

What mattered most to Jinjing when I met her was having a happy family life with her husband and son. That was also important to her before she went abroad, but now she saw the source of that happiness as being content with what she had rather than following the crowd, striving for more money and position.

Although Jinjing now saw the Bible as an important book about love, her worldview had not fundamentally changed. She might sometimes think about the existence of God, but she didn't have what others described in this book have. She didn't have a new identity: an identity as a child of Father God, a sinner saved by Christ—with a changed destiny, a new "family," and a shared story.

Xiaodan: Real Love, Real Life

Xiaodan was thirty-three and had been back in China nearly four years. She had married since her return, and was working as a secretary in a church. Xiaodan's husband, Chang, was a medical doctor who actively shared his faith She helped him disciple medical students.Since we met, Xiaodan and Chang have become parents and church leaders.

When I asked Xiaodan to divide her life into chapters, she included (1) childhood; (2) college; (3) working and first contact with Christ; (4) struggling and escaping; (5) overseas, a light; (6) coming back; and (7) a more peaceful life. She highlighted the struggles in her earlier life and pointed out that she identified two distinct phases in her Christian life, one as only a nominal Christian and one later with a completely new life.

A Hard Childhood: "I'm a stupid girl"

Xiaodan's parents were members of a generation who experienced hunger and poverty. Although life was better when Xiaodan was born, she grew up knowing what it was like to have very little money—for example, her parents couldn't afford to buy any cake or candy at all. Her mother worked hard selling snacks to support Xiaodan's education.

It was not her family's relative poverty, though, that made Xiaodan's childhood and early adulthood so desperately unhappy. Her father was violent toward her and her mother. He was a gambler and a very unhappy man. Xiaodan's parents were constantly quarreling, and she lived in fear:

> If I was studying or reading, he will come and like ..."What are you reading? You're such a stupid girl. Even if you read a lot, you're so stupid." He talked like this. So I was very scared. I didn't disturb him; I was just reading quietly so he won't come. Sometimes he would throw my book away. He had such a bad temper, so I was always very scared. Or he hit me. So I thought, "I'm bad; I'm bad." I told myself, "I'm not a good girl; I'm a stupid girl."

Her father's reputation and relationships with neighbors contributed to Xiaodan being bullied by other neighborhood children. Despite her mother's encouragement, she grew up comparing herself negatively with others. As a teenager, Xiaodan thought, "Oh, I'm so stupid, so ugly; and these girls are so beautiful. They are smart and have a decent family. Nobody will love me." It became hard for her to trust men.

Safety through success

Escaping her father became Xiaodan's sole aim in life. The best way to do so was by doing well enough in exams to get into a university away from her home city. She studied hard and was consistently top of her class. . This, along with her teachers' praise, gave her some confidence. Academic and career success, for

Xiaodan, became tied up with achieving safety—physical safety—and a sense of worth.

Before she left home for university, Xiaodan's only happy experiences were summer holidays, when she stayed with cousins in the country, and the knowledge that her mother loved her. But that was marred by her mother's unhappiness and inability to protect them both from Xiaodan's father.

University was twelve hours away by bus. Xiaodan was relieved to no longer fear her father's beatings. Although she enjoyed university life, deep down she was scared about the future. Her background gave her no family or security to rely on. "I was very scared in my deep heart, so the only thing I did was work very hard and continue to be the top student."

As an undergraduate, Xiaodan had her first encounter with church. There were more churches in that city than in most Chinese cities. At Christmas she and her friends thought going to church would be a fun thing to do.

> We just went there to experience the Western religion. I thought it was religion. So we went there and I got some food; they will give us some food, a package of oranges or candy, for Christmas Eve.

Xiaodan had a boyfriend at university. But after graduation she found work in that city and he did not. Their relationship ended, and she felt very lonely. She had an active social life , but most of it was spent drinking and complaining about life. She "did some stupid things" and developed "many bad habits."

Crisis and first encounter with Christians

Xiaodan continued straining to be the most successful at work, but she was very disappointed to discover that she wasn't good at her job. After three years of this unhappy post-university life, and feeling like an utter failure, Xiaodan lost all hope and became desperate. She questioned the point of all her efforts and her brave face. The world seemed "really ruthless."

During this crisis, Xiaodan met a Christian from her hometown. This woman took Xiaodan in and cared for her. She met other Christians and was struck by the contrast between their lives and her own. She started going to church, came to think of herself as Christian, met Chang, the Christian man who would later become her husband, and was baptized. She felt these Christians were special, so she wanted to be like them and enjoy their community life. Something, however, was holding her back:

> I was not so faithful. I still had ambitions in my heart, so I cannot be faithful. So it's like Christianity was a way for me to be together with decent people, to make sure I won't socialize with bad persons. Christianity was like a healing for me; but I could not devote myself completely to this belief, because I still had ambitions in my heart.

When she was twelve, Xiaodan had a vivid dream in which she met a foreigner and spoke with him in English. "There was a seed in my heart: 'you must learn English very well, because it will save your life in the future.'"

This grew into the idea of studying abroad. She shared this with the Christian lady, who encouraged her to study hard for the qualifying exams but also to pray for God to lead her. Xiaodan's understanding boyfriend also encouraged her to go and broaden her horizons.

Abroad: A new view of family, life, and love

Xiaodan was accepted onto a master's program related to her work in the health sector. She arrived on her new campus and everything was great. She felt free from worries, there was no pollution, and the people were nice. "Everything was new." She had saved, studied, and dreamed of going for so long and was not disappointed. She

Friends in China encouraged Xiaodan to find a good church. Soon after arriving, she visited a church and met a retired couple, Mary and Fred, who were to become very special to her. She also became friends with a Malaysian Christian "brother" in her program, who helped her academically. Both of them were welcomed into Mary and Fred's home and church cell group. To Xiaodan, they were "really like a family."

During this time, Xiaodan's view of life was transformed. She experienced family in a completely different way: special, harmonious, full of love. This gave her a new perspective on relating to others. She recounted it in the present tense, as she felt it when overseas:

> I feel like love is the most important thing in my life. You should love others. Because Mary loved, even though she had poor health. I feel, "They are Westerners but they care for me, they help me! So there's no reason for me not to love others." That is love from the Lord. Yes, I am completely changed.

Xiaodan's concept of what life can be, what her life could be, utterly changed as she experienced being loved and valued, and as she learned more about God. She learned to enjoy things for themselves—for example, cooking for others, learning about British history, reading novels.

> In China I was escaping life. This is "I'm enjoying life." This is so beautiful, living in such a harmonious family; so beautiful. This is true life; this is true love. "So what I expected before is wrong," I told myself. This is real life. Even if I worked very hard like before, in striving, competitive surroundings; even if I was very successful, very wealthy . . . I couldn't get such a peaceful heart. And this is real life, real life—not like before.

Because things were so wonderful, this was like a miracle to Xiaodan—and obviously all from God. She was so grateful to the Lord that she wanted to do something for him.

> Lord, you saved me from such a terrible surrounding to here. You purified me. I was a sinner before, because I was so disobedient. But you select me! I never expected I should get so many beautiful things. It's so beautiful, so happy, so peaceful. I never realized I can get it so easily from you, so I should do something for you.

The seed of a future ministry was sown. Over the years since then, Xiaodan and Chang have served the Lord by loving others. They share their home and the gospel with many young people, just as Mary and Fred did with her.

The return: "I am not God"

Despite being offered a job overseas, Xiaodan returned to China after her master's year. She had peace about returning and wanted to be near Chang. Also, before leaving China she had worked briefly in a hospital, and her boss had been kind to her. She heard the organization was struggling, so she returned to help.

Back in her old university city, Xiaodan became a senior manager in the hospital. Meanwhile Chang was studying in another city. Xiaodan was very successful at work, which she attributed to using Christian principles to manage people. She cared for the five hundred employees. Seeing that they had hard lives and little education, she provided training, opportunities to learn English, and a chance to join optional cultural classes. Many of them came to her with their problems.

For two years Xiaodan gave herself totally to her work. Her boss trusted her with financial decisions too. She stopped going to church; it took one or two hours to get there, and she needed to work on Sundays. Work was Xiaodan's life. She became distant from God, and this also led to arguments with Chang. Looking back on that time, she said she thought,

> "I can depend on myself, because look—I'm so successful, so many people trust me." I was like a god, because they did trust me at that time.

Eventually organizational politics became too much for Xiaodan. She saw people cheating others and didn't want to be like them. She also saw that people respected her for her power, not for herself.

> I feel God . . . in my life is a little bit disappeared, so I feel very weak. And I also feel like when people have lots of power, you can decide people's lives. I mean, if my boss tells me, "OK, Xiaodan, you can decide the salary of the whole department," they will look at you like God. If I cannot decide it, maybe they will not respect me as before.

The initial happiness wore off. Contrasting her life then with her relationships and life abroad, Xiaodan decided to leave her job, move near Chang, and return to church.

She went to work for a man who claimed to be a Christian. But he turned out to be a fraud, owing millions of yuan and firing people indiscriminately. He disappeared, leaving a wake of problems. And after three months, Xiaodan quit.

She was disillusioned and wary of working for another "Christian." Encouraged by her Chang, though, Xiaodan eventually took a secretarial job in a church. It took her a while to get used to the relatively low position, but when I met her she had been there a year and was happy, no longer struggling with her reduced status:

I really think it's the Lord's work. I feel very happy now, real happy.

Once again, Xiaodan contrasted her new "real" life with her old life—without Christ.

Marriage, church, and serving Christ

Soon after Xiaodan started the secretarial job she and Chang married. Looking back, Xiaodan realized that the reason she married relatively late for a Chinese woman, at thirty-two, was because she feared being in a marriage like her mother's. She was grateful to God that her marriage was totally different. Xiaodan loved helping Chang serve the Lord, by looking after him as he juggled a busy life as a medical doctor with ministering to students in their home and in the small church he started. Since I met them, they now also have children.

Xiaodan expressed sadness that so many of her friends, including returnees, were controlled by money. Their drive for material things had made them so busy that they had no interest in her experiences and no time to stop and think about life.

For Xiaodan, family and church life were intertwined. She was working as an administrator in a church, while she and her husband had started a small church where people could share their lives and experiences. She felt they had freedom to talk about all aspects of the Bible and about the work of the Holy Spirit, whereas some registered churches were more about "being good people."

For the time being their focus was on establishing churches in China, but they said serving abroad as medical missionaries was a future possibility.

Forgiveness and loving others

Xiaodan still struggled with some things. The atheistic denial of God that she was taught throughout her earlier life still surrounded her in the Chinese social context. Sometimes this caused her to use "human beings' logic"; but she kept praying that her mind would change.

Forgiveness was difficult sometimes too. Xiaodan said she had been through a lot, but God had given her peace, love, and the ability to forgive. She was very clear about her determination to love others, but also quite open about how difficult it is to really love some people:

> It's easy to talk about, but difficult to do. How can you love people, for example, who steal from you? It takes time.

Xiaodan asked, rhetorically, how she could forgive her father. She knew she *should* forgive him. And sometimes she *did* feel forgiveness for him. But up until when we met, she still sometimes had bad feelings about him.

Now that Xiaodan was secure in Christ, safe and loved by God, relatives and friends had observed that she seemed calmer and more confident. When people were angry or complained about her, she could stand back, remember that they are sinners, and then tolerate, forgive, and even love them. Xiaodan commented that this had to be real love, real calm, because people see through falseness.

I think this change is from God. You have to be tolerant, but you cannot pretend to be tolerant. You must forgive them from your heart. Even if they are very old, my response is "They are like a sinner; they are like my kid." You know, it's a very strange feeling; I treat them like a kid. They are so miserable because they don't have a place, a way, to vent, to complain. And they come to me, so God uses this opportunity. And they can tell, because they are mature people—they can tell if it's your true love or false love.

The change: Sharing real life, real love

I met Xiaodan on a Saturday, in her home. After the three of us enjoyed a simple lunch together, Chang took a nap. He needed to recharge after his hectic work week, before completing preparations for their Sunday meeting when they would share God's Word and love with student friends. They were replicating what Xiaodan received and learned through her time with Mary and Fred.

Since we met, they have continued. God has used them to bring the good news of real life and love, in Christ, to many more.

When I asked Xiaodan the best thing, or the greatest benefit, about being a Christian, she replied:

I think we cannot say "benefit." I just say "saved." We are saved, you know. It's like . . . alive. He selected me. I'm so blessed. So when I give the gospel to others, I know if somebody accepts the gospel, it's not from me; it's from God.

Xiaodan's life has changed utterly. The wannabe highflier settled happily into a lower status secretarial job, but is engaged with her husband in unpaid work of eternal consequence. The child and young woman who was desperate to succeed and be valued, who so much needed security, found security and much more. She found love, peace, purpose, and eternal life.

PART 4
The Change

6 What Mattered Most Before Belief

I walked around and looked carefully at your objects of worship. Paul in Athens

Acts 17:23

What we worship matters. Worshiping other gods—such as money, position, and security—places barriers between us and God. Valuing them more than our relationship with God gets in the way of eternal life. Our values matter.

It matters that we understand our own values, or "objects of worship." But we can also help *other people*—in this case, returnees—understand the values that drive their decisions, actions, and concerns. Then they can better understand the sin that enslaves and the freedom that Christ offers (Gal 5:1). They will be able to identify what habits and pressures are likely to divert them from following Jesus after they return to China. Old ways and old concerns are likely to pull them away if they aren't forearmed.

Identifying Values

I wanted to understand if and how my interviewees' core values had changed. To do that I had to help them look back over their lives. We were comparing what mattered most to them in the past, before they professed faith abroad, with what mattered in the present. I couldn't simply ask them what their values had been; few people would be able to answer that question at all, let alone objectively.

Values come into play when we face choices and difficulties; so dilemmas and major decisions are potential indicators of values. Our values are revealed by what we see as problems or conflicts, along with how we respond to them. Childhood relationships, especially with parents, are very important in shaping values.

Values can be seen in people's plans, ambitions, and hopes; in their attitudes toward money and their use of time; in their happiest and saddest memories; in the relationships that are most important to them. For new Christians, new or competing values can be understood by reflecting on tensions they face upon return. Values stemming from their Christian faith might also be identified by changes in which relationships are most important to them and in who influences their behavior.

To investigate whether people's values had changed while abroad and remained changed after their return, I talked to people who had been back in China at least one year. We looked back over their lives, from childhood through to their hopes for the future.

They shared their happiest and most difficult times, their past and current hopes. They described influential people, critical events, and big decisions. They talked about becoming Christians and about the tensions and joys of coming home and living as a Christian in China.

I took every opportunity I could to observe interviewees living out changed values: visiting in their homes, meeting family members, sharing meals, visiting the workplace of one and spending a two-day national holiday with another.

Patronizing their local shops and restaurants, or visiting their local park or university campus, gave me some feel for daily life. Using public transportation helped me appreciate why people find traveling a long distance to church on their only day off so exhausting. Visiting churches, and accompanying one returnee on her first visit to church, helped me appreciate some of the differences they encounter between churches abroad and in China.

I interviewed each person twice. In the first interview we talked about their lives chronologically, starting with their childhood, parents, and home settings and working through to the present time. The second interview focused on if, how, and why they had changed. Doing it this way helped people reflect on how their lives had developed.

I started by asking the interviewees to think of their lives as a book with chapters. Although some chose predictable headings (e.g., "school," "university," "UK," "work"), others' choices were more thought-provoking. Changlan, for example, chose only four chapters, but dedicated a whole chapter to life before primary school. His explanation for doing so was revealing.

Shared Values: Explaining the Tables

Each person had a unique set of values, but certain values were shared. Table 2 shows which values were held strongly by which individuals before they professed faith. Table 3 shows the strongest values after returning to China. The absence of an asterisk means the person didn't hold that value as one of their strongest, not necessarily that they didn't hold it at all.

The degree to which people shared certain core values was much greater after people became Christians than before.

Table 2: Values Held Strongly by Multiple People—Before

Name	Achievement	Admiration & Respect	Feeling Loved	Belonging & Camaraderie	Being a Good Child	New Experiences	Finding Purpose
Baozhai	x	x				x	x
Changlan			x		x	x	
Enci	x	x	x				
Fuyin	x	x	x		x		
Guang					x	x	
Huifang	x	x		x	x		
Jiang				x		x	x
Jinjing	x		x			x	
Ling				x	x		
Luli	x		x				
Mingzhu				x		x	
Qingzhao	x		x	x			
Ruolan	x	x				x	
Song	x	x		x			x
Xiaodan	x	x					
Xifeng	x	x	x		x		
Xing	x	x		x			
Xue			x	x	x		x
Yan	x	x	x				
TOTALS	13	10	9	8	7	7	4

Table 3: Values Held Strongly by Multiple People—At Time of Interview

Name	Caring for Family	Salvation / Closeness to God	Caring for Others	Honoring God	A Good Church	Gratitude & Contentment
Baozhai	x	x				x
Changlan	x	x	x	x	x	
Enci	x	x	x	x	x	
Fuyin	x	x	x	x	x	
Guang	x	x	x	x	x	x
Huifang	x		x			x
Jiang	x					
Jinjing	x		x			x
Ling	x		x			x
Luli	x	x	x	x	x	x
Mingzhu	x					x
Qingzhao	x	x		x	x	x
Ruolan	x	x	x	x	x	x
Song	x	x	x	x	x	
Xiaodan	x	x	x	x	x	
Xifeng	x	x	x	x	x	
Xing	x	x				
Xue	x	x	x	x	x	
Yan	x	x		x	x	x
TOTALS	19	14	13	12	12	10

Values before Professing Faith

So what were people's values, or "objects of worship," before learning about Christianity and professing faith abroad? They are presented here in descending order, starting with the value shared by the most people.

Academic and career achievement

Everyone had been driven by the need to excel at school—specifically, to score higher than others in the three key exams: middle school, high school, and university entrance. Xing said this struggle started in primary school and eventually involved up to eighteen hours of study a day. "The only purpose of our life was to pass the national university test, and to get a higher mark in the test. That was the only, only purpose."

Qingzhao described the pride she had felt in always being a top student. She recalled visits, as a teenager, to the Buddhist temple with her mother to pray for good grades. Yan mentioned her former pride at being the top student and then becoming a lawyer; progressing up the career ladder had been her sole reason for studying abroad.

Six of these driven achievers shared childhood memories of financial hardship; three mentioned highly driven parents. Jinjing and Fuyin studied for undergraduate degrees while continuing full-time work. And while Jinjing described a happy home life, other women, like Luli, Xiaodan, and Fuyin, directly attributed their earlier determination to succeed to unhappy childhoods.

Enci thought her father saw her and her education as an investment for future financial return. This attitude was not unusual in her part of China. Her parents' fights and her father's constant undermining of Enci's achievements led her to decide that security lay in career success rather than in the family. To become a "shining" businesswoman, she majored in both English and international trade in college.

Being admired and respected

Ten people previously really prized being admired by others. Nine women mentioned the recognition that came with being the top student as their happiest childhood memory. Others described their pride at being nominated as class monitor or president. Baozhai had enjoyed being admired at school when, as the top student, she was chosen for the Communist Youth League.

Desire for respect and status was reflected in decisions made about jobs. Fuyin hunted for a job in the UK, worried that returning to China without having worked abroad would cost her too much face. Xiaodan's story demonstrates how intense the desire for admiration can be and illustrates the insecurity that can drive it. It also showed how she came to see admiration as a false god.

Xing's happiest childhood memories were being a table tennis champion and being chosen chairman of the students' committee. His happiest time at university was being captain of the soccer team. His comments about his choice of university degree and of law as his profession revealed his enjoyment of intellectually challenging discussion and working out solutions to problems;

they also suggested a desire to impress and influence others with his intellectual abilities. Even after Xing's return, when he worked for a Hong Kong law firm on the mainland, he compared himself with his peers working in mainland-owned Chinese law firms, saying his was "a good job in their eyes, so I felt happy about this."

For Huifang, being respected for proper behavior was very important—apparently in relation to the memory of her late parents. Being physically, emotionally, and intellectually strong had been very important to her. As a master's student, she enjoyed representing her university in the long jump. As she advanced in her career, she took on a huge workload. Already a busy professor running a key laboratory, she took on her husband's lab too, because his professorial role required much travel.

Feeling loved

Love is different than admiration. Luli attributed her "love-seeking" and search for a man with a million yuan to an unhappy relationship with her parents. Sadly, another young woman had gone to the extent of harming herself when her mother told her to end her relationship with her university boyfriend. She wanted to be with the boyfriend she loved, but couldn't do that without distressing the mother she also loved.

Qingzhao was with her university boyfriend for two years. Initially she saw him every day; her parents even attributed her failure in the Chinese master's entrance exam to the relationship. Gradually they grew apart. Later, as a new Christian, she went out with a Muslim, but then gave up the relationship because she felt it would "hurt Jesus."

The importance of feeling loved came through more positively in Jinjing's description of her happiest childhood memories. She spoke vividly of a kind father who told her stories on summer nights and waited by the gate for her after school.

Sometimes something is most valued when it is in short supply. For four women, their prior desire for love stemmed from a childhood in which they didn't feel loved.

It wasn't only women who valued love. Changlan contrasted the love he felt before starting school with the lack of love he felt afterward.

Belonging and camaraderie

Song was the oldest of five children. At university, miles away from her home on the other side China, she missed her family, friends, and boyfriend so much. In five months, she wrote them 160 letters.

Huifang's happiest childhood memory was a building project in primary school in which she moved piles of bricks with classmates. The project was seen as hard-working and patriotic. Xue, however, said that as a child she always felt like she was "from another planet"; she even wondered if she was adopted. At university, and when she started working, she felt like she didn't belong. When Xue first believed in Christ, she feared that God might not have "chosen" her.

As an undergraduate in China, belonging and camaraderie made Jiang really happy. He was in a small university in which everyone knew each other and were "like older brothers and sisters."

Then there was the loneliness involved with being an international student. Xing admitted to crying when he first arrived because he missed his family so much. Jiang divided his time doing a PhD overseas into two distinct experiences. The difference wasn't just linked to his wife's coming to join him. He also experienced a whole "new world" of friends, and feeling like family, when they started getting to know local Christians. They even lived with a local family while awaiting the birth of their son.

> I think we got in a new world, which is in the same city but in a different, you know, dimension. And everything, every view, changed for me.

Being a good child (filial piety)

Filial piety was dramatically expressed by the young woman mentioned above who harmed herself during quarrels with her mother over a boyfriend. What made her pain so intense was her strong sense of duty to her parents. Unsurprisingly, she included this as one of three major milestones in her life. The others were when she failed the university entrance exam and had to repeat her last year of high school rather than allow her parents to borrow money to pay to get her into university, and when she became a Christian abroad. While the latter was an extremely happy time, the former provides another example of the importance of filial piety. wasn't driven to repeat the year and study hard just by concern about her parents' finances, but also by concern about their relationships with other people and their standing in others' eyes. It was a face issue.

> I wanted them to be proud of me. I didn't want, when people talk about me in front of other people, they feel ashamed or disappointed. It was my responsibility to glorify them, to make them look good in front of other people.

Huifang provided a very different example of filial piety. At twelve, she took on the responsibility of looking after her siblings while her mother stayed with her father when was in the hospital after a stroke. Later, Huifang was very conscious of the great effort made by her mother, despite her own poor health, to allow Huifang to continue to master's level while her younger siblings still needed funding for their education. She told me how she helped her mother have the best possible treatment; then, after her mother's death, she supported her siblings financially. Huifang takes her role as the senior woman in the extended family very seriously. Part of what drives her to do this is her desire to honor her mother's memory.

Huifang also revealed an intense desire to be respected. Failing to get into one of the top universities in China was the biggest disappointment of her teenage life. She had given much time and money to help members of her extended family get into university. Huifang felt a strong sense of duty to fulfill family and other relationships in a way befitting her place as the oldest child and a university professor.

Filial piety can extend beyond relationships with parents to seeing "one's life as an extension of one's parents' lives."[74] The Chinese honor their whole family through their social position and behavior.

Having new experiences

Experiencing new ideas, activities, and cultures was essential to seven people. Since all the interviewees had studied abroad, we might expect this to be important to everyone. Others' reasons for studying abroad, however, were more related to parental suggestion, seeking career advantage, or just observing others doing it. These seven relished discovering the world outside of China and experiencing new challenges.

Baozhai loved studying English as an undergraduate in China; she devoured English-language novels and watched films to learn about American and British culture. Language was "a door to another world," and her studies provided "a picture to see the lives, to see the history of Western people."

Jinjing enjoyed reading translations of classic foreign novels. This and her job as an English teacher fueled a dream to travel abroad. In her forties, she realized that dream as a visiting scholar. What she enjoyed most was learning about the culture and traveling around the country.

Jiang read about Oxford and Cambridge as a boy. When he eventually applied to one of them he wasn't doing it to get a better job afterward. He just wanted to be there, studying in this mythical place. More romantic still was Jiang's decision, against all advice, to marry a young woman from a different ethnic background—whom he had never even met! He met her father while traveling on business, and what people said about his daughters intrigued Jiang because it contradicted his ideas of what people in remote provinces of China were like:

> I thought, "Ah, in this place like a desert there are still some girls who have similar dreams like city girls in Beijing!" I was very shocked, because I thought this place was so rough and the people here so remote—and they share the same feelings as us!

Guang worked on a children's newspaper when he was in school and then won a job as a radio disc jockey at university. When I asked him why he stopped DJing after only two years, he replied:

> If I'm spending all my life in here . . . it's just like I can see all my future. But I don't want that. I don't want something you can predict. I'm still only in my twenties but I already know how all my life is going to spend? No, I'm not going to do that.

---

74   Kwang-Kuo Hwang and Kuei-Hsiang Han, "Face and Morality in Confucian Society," in *The Oxford Handbook of Chinese Psychology*, ed. Michael Harris Bond (Oxford: Oxford University Press, 2010), 479–98.

Guang didn't want all his life mapped out in front of him; he wanted surprises and fresh experiences.

Ruolan's desire for more in life led her to study in both Singapore and the UK. She expressed something similar. She couldn't bear to see everything laid out in front of her. Against her parents' advice, she left her secure engineering job to do graduate study:

> I wanted something more challenging. If I kept that kind of life, I could easily just think about the time I retire.

Finding Purpose

Xue left China consciously looking for the purpose of her life.

Baozhai's search for meaning and truth deepened after studying Mao Zedong thought as a Communist Youth League member at school. She wanted a "road" to follow. As an undergraduate in China, however, Baozhai started to have doubts about communism, especially when she met a foreign Christian teacher. She felt lost—meeting someone she respected but whose beliefs were contrary to all she held dear. Baozhai started questioning what she believed. She joined a Bible study group and started "knocking on the door."

As a child, Song pondered her place in the world:

> I thought about these questions frequently. It wasn't really clear, like a God or something like that. I just thought about . . . What was the earth like? Also, what is my position in this?

When Song was twelve, these questions disappeared in the pressure to succeed at school. Then she achieved everything she had been focussed on for the past thirteen years: she got into university. Away from home, she no longer had the role of big sister to four siblings. She felt "lost," with her heart "like an empty box." Then Leslie Cheung, a famous singer, committed suicide by jumping from the top floor of a hotel in Hong Kong. Song said she had "many illusions" and even wondered if the same thing could happen to her. Her depression deepened. She only recovered months later when she went home for vacation. She had been overwhelmed by a fearful sense of pointlessness.

While Jiang was in the UK, struggling with his PhD studies and missing his wife, he found a spiritual guide in the life and writing of the eminent economist Yang Xiaokai. Before becoming an economist, Yang became famous during the Cultural Revolution. He published an article entitled "Whither China?" and was imprisoned for ten years. Jiang based his PhD on Yang's economic theory, which Jiang thought was "noble." He was also attracted by Yang's life: his heroism in writing the article, his subsequent journey through severe hardship, his academic success in Australia, and his conversion to Christianity. Jiang drew parallels between Yang's life and his own: "I was his follower."

Would Other Chinese Students Have Similar Values?

These values won't be true of all Chinese students. However, having met many and having listened to the reactions of people who have heard my findings, I think what I have found will be true for many others.

I'd love to do similar research with a group of today's younger students. I might find different values. But then again, I might not.

7

What Mattered Most After Return

> *Sing to him a new song; play skillfully, and shout for joy. In him our hearts rejoice, for we trust in his holy name.*
>
> Psalm 33:3,21

The nineteen individuals I interviewed had all been back in China for at least one year. Did following Christ impact their values after their return? Yes, it did, when they really were following Christ. You can see from Table 3 on page 114 that twelve of the nineteen interviewees shared the three values most obviously related to Christian faith: salvation and closeness to God, honoring God, and being in a good church. . Their "object of worship" had indeed changed. The following are the values most common across the whole group.

Caring for Family

Relationships with parents and husband or wife were important to everyone. The family values expressed after conversion, however, were usually different than the filial piety before. Previously the interviewees had accepted apparent obedience to parents as the norm; now they engaged more actively with parents, stressing gratitude and care over obedience.

While pleasing parents had been their top priority before they believed in Christ, afterward several described actively going against parental wishes: in job decisions, church activities, or marriage. They were still in close contact with their parents and actively concerned for their well-being, but a new hierarchy of authority was in place. When parents' wishes conflicted with biblical teaching or what the interviewees believed to be God's wishes, they put God first. Ling was an exception; having a peaceful relationship with her parents eventually overrode going to church.

For the four single women in the group, the main authority figures in their lives beforehand were their parents. This was still the case for Ling, while the others valued divine approval more than parental approval.

For example, Xue's father had always made big decisions for her, and he was still involved in *some* decisions. When I met Xue, he had just committed her to pay the mortgage on a larger apartment, without even consulting her. However, since Xue had made the *biggest* decision of her life—to become a Christian—without consulting him, she had a different attitude. She submitted to her earthly father about the apartment because it didn't endanger her relationship with her heavenly Father. But in the matter of choosing a husband, Xue determined only to marry a Christian, despite this upsetting her parents.

Xue and others were concerned that their parents and other relatives came to believe in Christ. Relatives of six had already done so. Yan and Song each had a younger sister who had been baptized. Luli's mother had professed faith, and Luli now hoped her sister would too.

Thirteen talked about positive differences their faith in God had made in family relationships, despite tensions. Fuyin had been able to forgive her father for his treatment of her as a child. Though Enci had previously struggled to communicate with her mother, she led her mother to Christ and was now a great spiritual and emotional support for her.

Changlan and Guang appreciated their parents more since living abroad. The process of aging and acquiring responsibilities probably contributed too. They spent time with their parents. Guang repeatedly mentioned his gratefulness to them and his admiration for them. I couldn't tell if his appreciation was simply a result of maturity and the opportunity for reflection that distance from them had provided, or if his Christian faith contributed. Nevertheless, Changlan's faith clearly contributed to him valuing family very highly; and he criticized his former attitude. Talking about his teenage difficulties with his parents, he said:

> I started to have my own mind, and I felt my attitude toward the world is quite different from theirs; because I thought they were confined in a little world, and their sky is only that big. It was bad, actually. After I became a Christian, I thought that kind of thought was not good; it was not out of love.

The interviewees' faith affected their marriages too. Fuyin and Luli both attributed the survival of their marriages to prayer and to God making them more grateful and less self-centered. Six married women said that part of the wife's role is to support the husband. They mentioned this as something specifically Christian.

Ruolan, for example, had found that following her church's teaching about the wife submitting to the husband's leadership had led to reduced quarreling. (She said that although her husband wasn't always right, if she left him alone rather than argue with him, he eventually discovered that he was wrong!) Ruolan said she now thought of herself as having a special role in the family. Her self-concept had changed, and with it her values; she no longer put work first.

> In the past, I think work is the top. But now I think first is my family role, and then the job. Job is just the kind of way to support my life. I need to make a sacrifice for the family. Although I still sometimes got ambition to have a good position, sometimes I think I need to make a sacrifice.

Yan was trying to trust her husband rather than control him. She referred to Paul's words in Ephesians 5:25 about husbands needing to love their wives in the same way that Christ loved the church—that is, sacrificially; so the submission is two-way.

Eight interviewees had children, four more were either pregnant or hoping to become pregnant, and two others shared about their hopes for children and how they would raise them. One prayed regularly with her five-year-old daughter, who knows the whole Bible story and has told it to a friend.

One of Xing's reasons for becoming self-employed was to spend more time with his son. "Parents are the first teacher in front of their children. So I plan to teach him the Bible, to teach him what is the real meaning of life."

The interviewees' conviction to follow biblical teaching affected their parenting: for example, Ruolan's commitment to come home from work by five to be with her son, and Yan's sacrifice of a legal career to care personally for her children.

Of course, many saw church friends as family too; we will see more about that in chapter 9.

Salvation and Closeness to God

This spiritual element was very important to fourteen of the nineteen interviewees. When they shared about making big decisions or going through difficult experiences, they mentioned feeling saved by God, safe because of him, loved by him, or close to him. They described God actively caring for them.

Only Jinjing did not mention the importance of being in a relationship with God. She thought the Bible was a wonderful book about love and that Christians experienced and transmitted God's love, but she didn't believe God took a personal interest in her and she didn't think of herself as a Christian. Four others provided little evidence of closeness to God.

Enci was one of those with a close relationship with God—like "father and daughter." Although she had grown up feeling unvalued by her human father, she described God as

> a father who really cares, supports, and understands me. Even though I chose
> the wrong way to go, he was patient enough to wait for my return or remind
> me, not in a passive way. So every time I pray, I call him "Dad."

For Xue and Fuyin, believing that God loved them helped them know they were of value, despite their parents not appearing to value them. God's love made other women feel safe—both now and eternally.

Enci changed her work pattern because closeness to God was so important to her. She had been working until nine or ten o'clock every night, but started feeling distant from God. She resisted peer pressure and started leaving work at six thirty.

> This [work pattern] is not good for the relationship between me and God. I
> didn't have time for him. Even though I prayed wherever I am, or whenever I
> want, but it's just lacking something.

Qingzhao even called one of the chapters of her life "Saved." Woven through her story was the theme of needing to be close to God. She described being in a cycle of closeness and distance:

It's like you get closer to him and you leave him and you get closer to him and then leave him. But the degree is different; every time you leave him and you come back again, you will get closer.

Qingzhao saw God as the constant, faithful partner in the relationship:

It is like God has guided me all the time, although I'm not a good child. But he is loving me all the time.

It wasn't only the women who valued being close to God. Guang hoped to marry and said that being a good model for his children was his biggest hope. He felt he wouldn't be able to do that without God giving him the strength. It was as if there was an invisible cord between him and God:

I just don't want to be lost again, or disconnected, detached from him again.

Understandably, when I asked about any "benefits" of being a Christian, some mentioned salvation and the hope of eternal life. Laughing at her choice of words, Enci referred to "the sure ticket of entering the kingdom." Even in this life, with its difficulties, Enci has joy and peace from God.

Caring for Others

Knowing that God cared for them enabled the interviewees to care about the well-being of others. Increased awareness of their own sinfulness and shortcomings made them less judgmental and more patient with others.

Caring for others *beyond the family* is noteworthy in a culture that doesn't stress caring for people outside the in-group. I identified five common aspects to this new focus on others: increased understanding of others' perspectives, and a desire to take them into account; increased tolerance and forgiveness; greater focus on helping others; wanting to tell others about Christ; and serving in the church.

Before, Xiaodan quickly judged and pigeonholed people. Now she was more open:

When I view people, I use a different perspective. I try to understand why he does this, why she does that.

One of Xiaodan's work colleagues tended to treat other staff harshly. Before, Xiaodan would have been highly critical. Now she understood the unhappiness that caused her colleague's behavior and was trying to help her. I asked Xiaodan if she thought her increased empathy and tolerance was a result of maturity and living in another culture. She replied that the calmness, understanding, and forgiveness all came from God.

Ruolan now connects her former loneliness with having the wrong "attitude to life." She had spent all her time and effort in studying and climbing the ladder rather than in building relationships. It was all about getting to the best high school and best university. But God had given her hope and taught her "how to get along with other people, how to work, to have the right attitude toward your life, your work with other people." She had learned to think from other people's perspectives.

And because Ruolan now saw her own selfishness, she had stopped automatically seeing others as enemies or competitors. For instance, she had been angry about what she saw as her former supervisor's unreasonable behavior. Now, however, Ruolan could see that she had been at fault herself; she understands the supervisor's point of view. Ruolan's values have utterly changed.

> Something is important that I thought before is not so important. Something I thought is not so important, now I think is very important. To have harmony with other people is very important. [What is not very important is] to have a very good position.

Several people described improved tempers and an increased ability to forgive others. The sister of one returnee told me her sister's temper had improved as a Christian and she had better solutions to problems.

A desire to help others rather than to earn a high salary was reflected in job choices. Luli worked as a human resources consultant because she hoped to improve the way workers were treated. Xifeng was working for an NGO helping migrants rather than in a better-paid job teaching English, which her parents would have preferred.

Seven interviewees were actively sharing the gospel with people. Three others hoped their behavior would attract others to investigate Christianity. Enci saw missionary work as a probable part of her future. She contrasted that with her teenage years when she thought money would bring security. Referring to Mark 8:36, she said, "If I earn the whole world, and lost my life, what is the benefit of it?"

> The most important thing is that I want to live life for Jesus. If I have the chance, I want to share Jesus with them. I can see so many people are living in despair, living in disappointment. They need Jesus. They do need him.

Honoring God

Within "honoring God" I include faithfulness, obedience, and serving God; wanting to live in a way that reflects well on God; and wanting to do things God's way rather than depending on other means.

Obeying biblical commands was important. Changlan linked the improvement in his relationship with his father to the commandment to "honor" parents. Changlan, Enci, and Luli avoided jobs that would involve lying to customers or denying belief in God. In doing so, Enci and Changlan also placed fulfilling God's wishes above fulfilling their fathers' wishes. In both cases the father proposed using his connections to get his adult child a secure government job, but Enci and Changlan declined the help.

Enci still encountered dishonesty to customers in her foreign-owned firm, but challenged her boss about it. She considered God's opinion more important than that of her boss, who thought her naïve. Despite concerns about the consequences, Xue acknowledged her Christian faith on a registration form for a government job; she also upset her colleagues by refusing to falsify a tax claim.

Xifeng described what led her to work for a charity helping migrants. Before she studied abroad, she intended to return, find a job, "earn a lot of money," and "make my parents proud." After becoming a Christian, she acquired a different perspective:

> I realized my life is not only about job, about money, about making my parents proud (look good in front of other people, I mean). There is meaning in your life. Now I've found it. It's Jesus. It's like you've finally found your creator. You've finally found out why you are living in this world.

Marrying a Christian was important to most. The way Xue managed her parents' pressure to marry was described earlier. Here's what Qingzhao shared about breaking up with her Muslim boyfriend:

> I know I hurt God; I know it's wrong. I can't hurt Jesus like that, so I decided to give up that relationship. That was very painful, but I know that was right, that was the right thing to do. So I did that and came back to China. I think the love for God, Jesus, helped me to do that. That was the main thing. It's like I'm practicing Christianity. It has helped me.

Yan had her first child in the UK and now sees this as part of God's plan for her and her husband, so that they would stay longer in the UK and become Christians. Having completed her degree and run out of money, but with the offer of a high-paying job back in China, Yan unintentionally became pregnant again. She described the struggle over whether to have an abortion and take the job (the expected response in China) or to keep the baby and give up the job:

> We can't see blessing at the time; we struggle; we have the financial problem. We need to go back, to have money, very soon. And my husband needs to start from the beginning because he gave up all the clients to go to UK.

Yan and her husband chose to keep the baby rather than the high-status, high-paying legal job, because they saw God as the ultimate authority in their lives:

> I didn't think too much. We just fear God; we fear God. We don't dare to do that. We don't dare do the abortion. At first it is the fear. And then . . . we know that's the blessing. It must be something in the future.

In China, when their second child was a year old, Yan felt ready to go back to her career—only to find she was pregnant again! This was very serious, because it was acceptable for a couple who had studied and given birth to a child abroad to have a second child, but not a third. So that her daughter would have identity papers, Yan flew to a distant country that would accept the child as a national and gave birth there. Yan was initially very angry with God, and described having to tell the doctor that she wanted to keep the baby, while feeling inside that she didn't want her.

Do you know that, the struggling inside? I know I can't have an abortion, but I really don't want this baby.

Foreign friends told Yan that to have one child was a "blessing'" but having three was even more blessing; but she just felt "a lot of pressure." However, she and her husband were committed to obeying God. Yan sees the blessing now: by giving them the children, God changed their direction and led them to see the better life for them. Others also described doing things God's way as a struggle to give control to God, which resulted in peace.

Two people showed little sign at all of thinking that God was interested in them. Since returning to China, Huifang had declined to join colleagues burning incense in temples. However, she said her busy work schedule and supporting her husband's career prevented her from attending church and made Bible reading difficult.

Jinjing was not attending church, and her comments revealed that she didn't fully understand the gospel or think of herself as a Christian. Nevertheless, the Bible spoke to Jinjing enough for her to develop a module for her students regarding the significance of the Bible upon Western culture.

Being Part of a Good Church

Eleven of the nineteen returnees regularly attended church services and spent time in church activities. A twelfth had fellowship with Christians at work. The "family" aspect made church crucial for them: they had close relationships with like-minded people who were a source of emotional and spiritual support. Intimacy arose from shared identity, values, and purpose. As one of the men, Guang, put it: "We're sharing. We're emotionally connected." They met at least weekly with other Christians.

For these people a "good church" was also where the whole of the Bible was taught accurately, in ways that helped their daily lives. They commented on how both preaching and personal Bible reading affected their lives. Changlan, Enci, and Fuyin referred regularly to specific parts of the Bible to illustrate points they were making.

Song's life illustrates how church fulfills three needs: to have close relationships with other Christians, to understand the Bible, and to serve others. Although this twenty-six-year-old married woman worked for an investment company, she spent much of each weekend and several evenings a week in church activities. On Tuesday evenings she met with others to pray and study the Bible. Another evening she read the Bible with a new believer. On Saturday evenings Song and her husband joined the church prayer meeting, staying overnight with other church members and then rising early for prayer before the Sunday morning service, which was followed by lunch. Once a month she took part in an outreach event.

Five were in church leadership positions. Xue helped lead a church of more than two hundred. In addition to teaching and pastoral and organizational responsibilities, she was taking a Christian counseling course and translating Christian books. She also had a full-time secular job. Xue's criteria for deciding whether a church was good were that they were faithful to the Bible and that she could see God was with them

Seven of the eleven who attended church regularly were in house churches, two were in registered churches, and two went to both registered and house churches. People gave similar reasons for going to unregistered churches: they placed importance on understanding Scripture to live their lives well.

One woman initially thought she might get into trouble if she went to a house church, but she went anyway because she had heard that registered churches weren't allowed to teach certain parts of the Bible. She wanted "to go to some place they could freely speak God's Word." Another said that if she went to a registered church she would not receive "real meat." A third was a regular member of a registered church, attended a small home-based group for returned students, *and* sometimes went to an unregistered church because the Bible interpretation was more "sophisticated" and all parts of the Bible were taught. She said registered churches were unable to teach the resurrection and second coming of Christ adequately and were more focused on teaching people to be "good" and "not to make any trouble."[75]

One man didn't want to identify as either a "house church Christian" or a "registered church Christian," but simply as "a Christian." He saw the registered church he goes to every Sunday as *his* church; his wife is in the choir and they both take part in a fortnightly meeting of young married couples. He contributes there, has close friendships there, and has been helped and encouraged there. He also went to a house church, famous for its minister and Bible teaching. He explained, "In family churches, seems the topics are more open. And the message I can get there is a little bit different from what I can get in the government churches."

One woman moved to a house church because she found her registered church too big and impersonal. The two who attended two churches for several years have now settled into just one: one in a different house church, the other in his original registered church.

Being part of a good church was not valued by everyone. The seven who did not have "honoring God" as a strong value were not attending church when I met them. Xing initially helped lead a group for people exploring Christianity, but he had not been for about a year, since his wife became pregnant. He spoke of his trust in God and his plans to return to the group, but his overriding current concern seemed to be the health and financial and emotional well-being of his family.

Three people appeared never to have seen a great need for church. Jinjing had never even visited, giving as reasons the distance to the only church she knew of and family and work commitments. Huifang went to church once, only to find it locked; she had emailed contacts given her by another returnee, but said these people had not replied. At least two other factors were probably at play. Both ladies live in cities where church buildings are less obvious than in

---

75   These experiences and opinions will not apply to everyone. Church practice varies in China. For example, I have heard the Second Coming mentioned in a registered church sermon.

some cities, and neither city is known to have numbers of intellectuals interested in Christianity.[76] The opportunities for them to find people with a similar background would be more limited. Also, both women went overseas for only one year and seemed to have a more limited understanding of the Christian faith than others.

Although Baozhai visited a Christian returnee group a few times and attended a Bible study at her workplace a couple of times, she said she didn't feel it was necessary to be in a group to be with God. She too seemed to have a limited understanding of Jesus as Lord and Savior.

Gratitude and Contentment

Feeling safe with God and having hope in eternal life were usually accompanied by gratitude. Twelve interviewees said they had ceased to strive so much for success and the status symbols money can buy. Qingzhao had rejected working on Sundays in favor of attending church. This was despite the financial rewards of Sunday work and her mother's desire that she work hard to afford a larger apartment. Guang kept saying "I'm a lucky guy" and voicing appreciation for his parents and for God.

Even three ladies who didn't have a clear Christian faith were now more content. They attributed this both to experiencing a more relaxed lifestyle abroad and to their religious experience there. Jinjing was at pains to help me understand the driven nature of life in China. She wished her husband wouldn't work so hard.

Baozhai now placed less emphasis on getting a highly paid job that could bring status and material possessions.

> Yes, the country influenced me. As a religion, it doesn't matter what you will do, how high your job is. It matters that you do what you want to do and you do it well, to be yourself and to be helpful and influential to others.

Baozhai may have mixed biblical principles and Western individualism, but she credited God with having "released" her from her former desire to be perfect and to please others.

Even Huifang, whose life focused on hard work and sacrificing herself for others, was starting to think that maybe there was greater significance in being loved *by* God than in doing things *for* him. She said that before going abroad she visualized God as a "great man" who would love her if she worked hard to please him: "If I work hard, I spend every minute to work, work, work, to help the society, help our country, so I think the great man, the God, the great man, will love me."

But a Chinese Christian overseas told Huifang that hard work doesn't necessarily lead to God's love. She was now wondering whether she would do better simply to enjoy the life God had given her.

---

76   Beijing and Shanghai, for example, are known to have considerable numbers of university students and staff attending churches.

What Helped Sustain These New Values?

Value change varied between interviewees; so did the nature and degree of Christian faith. Twelve people shared the three values most obviously related to Christian faith: salvation and closeness to God, honoring God, and being in a good church. They shared a similar concept of themselves as Christians and held key elements of the biblical Christian account as their own personal story. They now saw God as the highest authority in their lives and valued serving, trusting, and being loved by God very highly—or rather, they simply valued God very highly. They no longer held academic and career achievement, being admired, and feeling loved as their strongest values, because they experienced a new identity as a child of God, with a new source of security.

The same twelve individuals maintained strong bonds with other Christians in a Christian community (church for eleven and a Christian workplace for one); eight of these were married to Christians. Also, aspects of their church experience abroad acted as a bridge to continuing in church life after their return. More about that later.

The remaining seven interviewees shared fewer of the particularly Christian values, nor were they at that time going to church. They lacked a community of people who shared a Christian story, identity, and values. Four of the seven had been baptized overseas. Three of these four had not settled in churches because they were concerned about government restrictions.

I believe that two of the seven whose values had changed less had never really understood the gospel and did not share the others' Christian identity and story. These two women, Huifang and Jinjing, were both academics who lived in cities with fewer visible churches. Nor had their husbands accompanied them abroad. They were not in contact with people who could encourage them to continue seeking.

The final person, Baozhai, had changed but didn't embrace all the Christian values shared by the twelve. Perhaps the changes within her stemmed from her experience living abroad and then her new life as a wife and mother, rather than from trust in Christ.

8 New Story, New Boss, New Identity

> *Do not conform to the pattern of this world, but*
> *be transformed by the renewing of your mind.*
> *Then you will be able to test and approve what*
> *God's will is.*
>
> Romans
> 12:2

"Who are we and what are we here for?" theologian Christopher Wright asked at the beginning of one of his books.[77] Starting to answer his own questions, he entitled the second chapter, "People Who Know the Story They Are Part of."

The returnees I know who have changed the most see themselves as part of that story and are living it out alongside other like-minded people. They have taken the biblical narrative as their own master story. It informs their own self-concept. It gives them a purpose: to play their part in their creator God's purposes—the God they now see as the ultimate authority.

Changed Master Stories in the Bible

Talking first to the crowd in Jerusalem (Acts 22) and then to King Agrippa (Acts 26), Paul recounts his prior life as a Pharisee and persecutor of Christians. He then describes his encounter with Christ and the changes that brought to his life. He does this to bring credibility to the account of humans' potential new relationship with God that he wants his hearers to share.

Paul, Peter (Acts 2), and Stephen (Acts 7) all summarize the history of the Jewish people and show how Jesus fulfills that history. They urge their hearers to acknowledge that Jesus fills major gaps in their prior understanding of themselves and of God, and then to repent and follow Christ. People need to accept this new account as their own story.

The apostles Peter, John, and Paul all write of Christian believers as having a particular identity: as being "chosen" (1 Pet 2:9); as being "children of God" (John 1:12; Rom 8:16); as having had their sins forgiven (1 John 2:12); as being a "new creation" (2 Cor 5:17) with purpose, such as bringing the message of reconciliation with God (2 Cor 5:18–20); and as having a glorious destiny (Rev 21:1–4). And this isn't merely an individual identity; the church is described as the bride of Christ (Rev 21:2); the body of Christ (Eph 5:30); a royal priesthood

---

77   Christopher J. H. Wright, *The Mission of God's People: A Biblical Theology of the Church's Mission* (Grand Rapids: Zondervan, 2010).

(1 Pet 2:9). These and many other passages in the Bible influence Christians' ideas of themselves—their self-concept.

Before Paul met Christ, his deepest value was to achieve righteousness himself by fulfilling the law (Phil 3:4–6). Afterward, what mattered most to him was "to know Christ—yes, to know the power of his resurrection and participation in his sufferings, becoming like him in his death, and so, somehow, attaining to the resurrection from the dead" (Phil 3:10,11).

Paul's words and actions revealed how much his master story, self-concept, and values had changed.

Returnees with Changed Master Stories

What do I mean by saying someone had a new master story and self-concept and recognized a different authority, a new boss? Here are three examples.

Luli

Luli grew up believing she needed to fight to support herself and her family until she found a man with a lot of money who would love her, bring her security, and solve her family's problems. That master story collapsed while she was studying abroad: she lost her boyfriend and his financial support, and simultaneously learned that her brother was dying of cancer. The crisis opened Luli to exploring Christianity, a different account of life, which she had glimpsed earlier, in China.

Luli attended a church where she heard clear, practical Bible teaching, and she also joined a mainland Chinese Mandarin-speaking home fellowship. She became an avid Bible reader and prayed regularly. She experienced friendship and sacrificial generosity from Chinese and British Christian friends. Life was a roller coaster, but God was at work—and Luli knew it.

The narrative Luli lived by changed: God existed, loved her, and could be trusted, even in severe difficulties. The idea that money and a rich husband was the answer evaporated. Soon after Luli returned to China, she married a man who was by no means rich, but he was a Christian. She sought a career in line with God's values and urged her family to follow Christ too. Previously, Luli herself and money were the authorities in her life; now God is her authority, accessed through the Bible and prayer with her husband and church friends.

Fuyin

In her spiritual journey, Fuyin believed first in the existence of God. She only understood the significance of Jesus' death and resurrection some six months later, after returning to China. An early milestone toward belief in God came when Fuyin read a book about archaeological evidence of events described in the Bible. This challenged her atheistic worldview. Maybe events in the Bible had really happened!

Then Fuyin's plan to work abroad failed and her marriage was a mess. Her self-concept as a strong, capable, respected woman with a high-paying job, a high position, and a happy family was smashed. Her worldview and master story likewise disintegrated. The crisis showed Fuyin that she needed God.

Talking about life since her return, Fuyin repeatedly referred to God: "God said this"; "God allowed that"; "God gave me peace"; "God hasn't used me yet"; and so on. The Lord was a constant presence in her life. Fuyin recounted the day she realized her husband was a gift to her from God, and she spoke of people she had met as having been sent to her by God so that she could help them know him. People were introduced to each other by God, for his purposes and their good. Her choice of *Fú yīn* (福音), meaning "gospel," as her alias for my research, illustrates her new purpose in life: introducing others to God. She was carrying tracts in her handbag in case she met someone who might benefit from them.

Fuyin's daily Bible reading and frequent listening to online sermons had made her quite familiar with the Bible. She referred to passages in both the Old and New Testament to illustrate situations in her own life; this was her story too.

Before, Fuyin was disillusioned with work and with relationships she thought were based on corruption and flattery. She saw life as a hard, lonely battle in which she could rely only on her own strength and success. Fuyin said, "I see myself differently now." She referred to herself as "God's servant" and talked about Christians needing to be "salt and light." She liked Mother Teresa's quote about being used by God like a little pencil to send a love letter to the world.

Xue

Unlike Luli and Fuyin, Xue did not have a crisis while studying abroad. She arrived actively seeking the purpose of her life, sensing there must be more to life than acquiring money and a nice house. Xue's worldview already included a God who had created the world, but her explorations of religion had not yet taken her beyond that.

Xue described her childhood as "loneliness" and shared that she grew up feeling like an outsider. When I met her in Beijing, she was no longer lonely. She was enjoying close relationships in church, felt loved by God, and had a clear purpose: to do God's work. As a girl, Xue had a vague image of serving someone important—and that was now reality! She enjoyed serving in various ways: leading a youth ministry, translating Christian books, and counseling.

Xue described herself as a "sinner, trusting in Jesus." She talked as though God was active in her life: recalling that he helped her find a church after her return to China, and saying that he was "training" her. Looking back, Xue described her time abroad as a new Christian as "full of God's grace," noting that God had put people in her path who helped her to grow in faith and to serve.

This new narrative was not just about herself. Recognizing that she had been "blind before," Xue said she could now see where humans come from and where we are going, and that she was looking forward to the future, to eternal life.

Relationship with God: A Recurring Theme

I didn't specifically ask the interviewees, "What is your master story or worldview?" Instead, I analyzed the transcripts of our conversations in great depth, looking for comments that illustrated a biblical or Christian worldview.

Themes appeared. At the heart of the story that twelve people presented as their personal master story was God, described as Father, with Christ as Savior. They described God's love, protection, power, and authority. God wasn't just seen as a *concept*; he was *acting* in their lives.

Qingzhao, for example, portrayed her relationship with God in which each time she became distant from him he would draw her back, even closer. Ruolan referred to God the Holy Spirit prompting her to check something in the Bible. Xifeng shared how the Holy Spirit moved her to apologize when she had been angry with God. They clearly thought of themselves in a personal relationship with God.

A New Self-concept: A "New Creation"

Salvation involves being "born again" (John 3:7) into new life in the Holy Spirit; not only is the person's perception of their identity changed, but also their actual identity. They are a "new creation" (2 Cor 5:17) and a child of God (Galatians 3:26). This new birth includes becoming part of the "kingdom of God" (John 3:3) and brings "living hope" (1 Pet 1:3).

For the interviewees, having a new explanation of life was related to a changed self-concept. This explanation included a powerful God who loved them, had saved them, and had purposes for them. So they saw themselves as loved children of God. The women who previously had very little sense of worth knew God had a part for them to play in his plans.

From time to time, though, the old ideas troubled some people. Three admitted to sometimes worrying that they might not be good enough for God. Usually they felt free and special, valued by God simply for being themselves. Occasionally, however, they felt pressure, as if another level of duty and obedience had been added—now to God, as well as to their parents. Xue provided a reason, explaining that sometimes her idea of God was confused by her experience of her earthly father, whom she portrayed as emotionally distant but controlling.

A New Source of Power, Authority, and Security

Seeing God as loving and powerful and themselves as saved impacted the interviewees' ideas about security. Some earlier values were rooted in a lack of security. Xiaodan, Enci, and Luli experienced childhoods lacking in paternal support. They sought financial independence as a way of escape from insecurities and pressures. They and Fuyin all mentioned anger and arguments in their childhood homes. And although Yan's parents didn't fight, she was separated from them for several years. She became very insecure, and then sought career success to give her control over life. Others described happy childhoods and loving parents, but the intensely competitive education system instilled the idea that security comes from being the highest achiever.

Sources of security changed after believing in Christ. None of the women mentioned above were still seeking security through career or financial success. One was unemployed, one was a full-time mother, one was working part-time as a church administrator, one had reduced overtime work to spend more time praying and reading the Bible, and the fifth had a very responsible though not particularly high-paying job and lived in a tiny apartment that reflected her income. They found their security in God, who provided for them and loved them in ways their earthly parents could not. Four had secure, happy marriages with Christian men; and the fifth was single and enjoyed a network of Christian friends. They found support in these relationships of shared story and values.

Xue, a single woman, had a complicated relationship with her controlling father. Although she sometimes felt frustrated that her father made important decisions for her, she also sometimes wondered how she would cope if he weren't there to help her. Believing that God was in control, and in control of her father, gave her peace of mind.

Previously, twelve had seen the main authority in their lives as either their parents or themselves. Now authority was seen to lie in God and the Bible. They believed God had their interests at heart. Formerly, strength was perceived to come from their own hard work, career achievement, and position. Now they saw giving up control to God as essential for their well-being.

This came across most vividly in Yan's explanation that fear of God led her not to abort her third pregnancy. However, her attitude toward God wasn't simply one of fear; she referred repeatedly to his blessings and how she now saw good resulting from her earlier difficulty. Being in line with God's will took precedence over career aspirations, financial security, and others' opinion of her.

Xiaodan allowed herself to become like a god to the staff in the hospital she managed, and later she fell victim to internal politics. The experience was tough but valuable. It humbled her; she recognized her own weakness and need to depend on God.

Eagerness to please and trust God was revealed in relationships with parents. Although Song still cared about her parents' feelings, when she made important decisions their advice came lower in the pecking order than before. She now sought advice first from the Bible and in prayer, then from her Christian husband and church leaders, and only after that from her parents. Changlan's rejection of his father's help finding a job is another example.

Commitment to church activities, prayer, and Bible study showed how people now looked to God as ultimate authority. Many stressed the importance of prayer, describing answers they had received. Xifeng described her ongoing conversations with God. Recalling how she began working for a Christian NGO, she interspersed comments about what happened with things she said to God:

So I sent out my CV and I was so looking forward to having this job. So I prayed, "God, I really want to do this job. I think because the job description— it's like kind of job you prepare for me." . . . I prayed, "Father, please help me, because I have been waiting this long. You know how many months. You know how anxious I am, how much I want a job." So I prayed; I prayed a lot. And the next day I got this interview call. And after the call, I felt the Spirit is cheering inside. So I prayed, I gave my thanks to God: "Oh, thank you; thank you so much."

Some Changed Less

Jinjing was impressed by the peaceful lifestyle of Christians overseas. Back in China she emulated the hospitality she had received abroad by inviting international students to her home. However, she did not adopt the biblical narrative as her own. Abroad, she had temporarily accepted explanations that the promises of the Bible were for Chinese people too. At home, though, without Christian friends, Jinjing said she thought the Bible was for "Jews and people from some other countries," but not for China. She no longer thought that God was interested in her, and she didn't consider herself a Christian. She revered the Bible as a book about love, but didn't read it for her own benefit.

While Huifang referred to herself as "Christian" while talking to me, she hadn't met with Christians in China and she talked of Jesus as being the one "big god" among many. She said she hoped to study theology in the future to find similarities between Christianity and Buddhism. I doubt that Huifang had a saving faith.

Though Baozhai appeared to have a changed self-concept after her time overseas, it wasn't clearly Christian. She referred to God as Father and herself as his daughter, saying she no longer felt the need to be perfect and no longer feared death. However, Baozhai saw no need to meet other Christians, saying that she didn't need other people to be with God. She didn't feel the need to read the Bible regularly. She made no reference to Christ, sin, or salvation. She had married since returning to China and referred to her husband as "sent" to her by God, but he was not a Christian.

Though Baozhai seemed grateful to God for giving her a good job, comfortable apartment, and happy marriage, she seemed unaware of the greater value of what Christ had done on the cross. Hers was a limited and individualistic idea of a relationship with God. She seemed to mix appreciation of a more individualistic lifestyle—free from pressure to live up to others' expectations— with Christianity.

Baozhai's most vivid church experience occurred shortly before she returned to China. At an Alpha Course day focused on the Holy Spirit, she experienced something that made a very strong impression on her. Others said they could *feel* God with them, and she wanted that experience too. "I think he [God] came to me at that time, and hugged me, and made me so hot and so heavy. So I was in, and he was there." Although this may have been a real encounter with the Holy Spirit, I'm afraid Baozhai interpreted this experience—rather than what

Christ has done—as the basis for her acceptance by God. Her comment that she 'was in' may indicate that she thought God had accepted her; or it could indicate that she felt she was now really part of that group of people.

Ling also seemed not to have changed as much as others. I saw the baptism testimony she wrote overseas; in that she mentioned human sin and the result of Christ's death on the cross.[78] She didn't mention Christ in our conversation, however, but just occasionally referred to God.

Ling said she wanted to be like the kind Christians she met overseas. She described her experience of a church in China, moving from place to place, as feeling like "thieves." It didn't fit her idea of how good people should behave.

Maybe what impressed Ling most during her time abroad was Christians rather than Christ. Or maybe she really had trusted in Christ for salvation, but found the pressures of life in China too great to continue in church.

---

78 I wonder how often what Chinese students say in baptism testimonies abroad is what they *believe* is the correct thing to say rather than what they have personally decided is true and to be followed.

9 New Family

> *"Who are my mother and my brothers?" [Jesus] asked. Then he looked at those seated in a circle around him and said, "Here are my mother and my brothers! Whoever does God's will is my brother and sister and mother."*
>
> Mark 3:33–35

God is building a people to be *his* people. That theme runs throughout the Bible. And it's a *people*, not a scattered bunch of individuals. Paul calls these people—this people—"the body of Christ" (Eph 4:1–16; Col 1:18). Peter describes his readers as "a chosen people, a royal priesthood, a holy nation, God's special possession" (1 Pet 2:9). He goes on to say: "Once you were not a people, but now you are the people of God" (v. 10).

Returnees who grow in their faith see themselves as part of this people. They speak of it as "family": themselves as children of Father God and other Christians as brothers and sisters. They echo the family language of passages such as Hebrews 2:10–13 and Romans 8:1–17.

Those who did not share the Christian master story held by the others were not attending church when I met them. They showed little sign of seeing themselves as part of God's kingdom or family. In turn, without such a community they lacked the stimulation, support, and relating of faith to life that encouraged the others to pray, seek guidance in the Bible, and see God at work—and to see themselves as part of the bigger picture.

For example, while Xifeng described how talking and praying with other Christians helped her feel close to God, Baozhai made no mention of Christ or salvation and saw no need to meet with others. While Guang and Ruolan shared how their Christian faith had grown in their Chinese churches, Jinjing, who had never been to church since returning to China, had readopted her pre-overseas position of thinking that Christianity was not for the Chinese.

A New Community

The returnees I know who are growing in faith and "producing a crop" are those who determinedly settled into a church. They are sharing their faith, experiencing improved relationships, bringing Christian principles to the workplace, and contributing to the church. They are seeking to glorify God in many areas of life. Following Fowler's definition of conversion, they have a "commitment to reshape [their lives] in a new community of interpretation and action."

Often this is not easy. It takes effort to find churches and get to know people. Difficult decisions must be made about the use of time. Family (or bosses!) may expect the returnee to spend Sunday with them rather than going off to join strangers. A new relationship with parents or other family members may need to be worked out in order to negotiate time with brothers and sisters in Christ. In some countries parents and children operate quite independently of each other, but in China that's rarely so. There the family relationship is by far the dominant relationship; it's unusual to have strong bonds with groups that aren't connected to either family or work.

Faith in Christ, and being part of the church, involves a different concept of home, family, and relationships. For a Chinese returnee, committing to a church can be like committing to a new family. This entails both blessings and tension. It may be essential for the believer's spiritual growth, but it may feel shameful and hurtful to his or her blood family.

"Family," In-group, and "Home"

The Chinese expression often used to refer to unregistered churches is *jiātíng jiàohuì* (家庭教会)—literally, "family church." Calling fellow believers "brothers and sisters" is normal among Chinese believers. It reveals a strong identification with a group. The desire to be part of an in-group is much stronger in Chinese culture than in individualistic Western cultures.[79] The in-group determines social behavior.

Ling felt uncomfortable about her church meeting in secret; it seemed less than respectable. On top of that, her parents didn't like her going. So she gave up attending church. She returned to the safety and respectability of her known in-group. The church she attended in China never became her trusted in-group, but her parents always had been.

Others fared better. The sense of belonging they received from being part of a church family in China helped them overcome initial tensions in their relationships with parents after they became Christians. Those married to Christians had their own little Christian in-group to sustain their Christian self-concept and values. Enci returned with a ready-made new in-group of close friends who were at the same overseas university and then attended the same church in China. Xue acquired a strong in-group in her Beijing church, possibly more easily because her family was never really her in-group. She had always felt on the family margins, even wondering if she was adopted.

Xifeng was involved in her overseas church to the extent of working as a church volunteer and living with a church family after graduating. When I first met her in China, she had not yet found a nearby church. She yearned to be in one, saying, "It's time to come home." For her, and others, the idea of "home" had changed. Initially she struggled to find such a home, or in-group, but later she did.

For some, the notion of home includes their church family in their country of study. That was where they first met God; and people there, the church

---

79   The term "in-group" is used by cross-cultural psychologists such as Harry Triandis.

community there, remain important to them. As one missionary said, returning to his birth country, "Home will always be defined a little more broadly now."[80]

The initial leaving can be more painful than we realize; for some returnees it is like mourning the death of someone close.[81] Many miss overseas Christian friends greatly. I was on the phone with a recent returnee who sounded uncharacteristically flat. This bubbly, outgoing young woman loved her overseas church so much that she proclaimed it "my church." She has committed to a church in China, but it will take time for her to feel she belongs. Right now she feels different, as she is the only one of her age. Her faith feels a bit strange too, probably because her life experience and road to faith is also different. She just finished university and has lived abroad; the church people are older, with children and grandchildren, and have not lived abroad.

Guang's experience was quite different. He found a church "home" in China quickly. He was able to relate to people there. "We're connected," he said. Some people avoid the degree of grief experienced by others because they see themselves as part of the international family of God: church is their family, whether they are overseas or in China. Their use of family language about church reminded me of Jesus' description of his disciples as "my mother and my brothers" (Mark 3:34, above, and Matt 12:49).

Blessings and Tensions in Relationships

Relationships with parents

It was moving to see how much those who had not felt loved as children had blossomed knowing that they were loved, valued children of God. It was also moving to hear how they were forgiving their parents and sharing the gospel with them. Theirs was not an individualistic gospel; they wanted their families to know it too. They understood their ministry of reconciliation within their families. Church teaching and encouragement helped them.

Four women described close church relationships that contrasted with their descriptions of unhappy childhoods. These new bonds and community provided security for those whose family relationships were broken or distant. Perhaps some were free to build strong bonds at church partly *because* the bonds with parents were so weak. Xiaodan's discovery abroad of what relationships could be like in a Christian family was still vivid to her. She took this back to China where she and her husband were reproducing this loving Christian family as they welcomed students to their home.

In many cases, family relationships had changed. Sometimes this was because the Christians were now focused less on themselves and more on others.

---

80 V. L. Hunter, "Closure and Commencement: The Stress of Finding Home," in *Cross-Cultural Reentry: A Book of Readings*, ed. Clyde Austin (Abilene, TX: Abilene Christian University, 1985), 188.

81 Andrew Butcher, "A Grief Observed: Grief Experiences of East Asian International Students Returning to Their Countries of Origin," *Journal of Studies in International Education* 6, no. 4 (2002): 354–68.

For two interviewees, the change probably arose from marrying and becoming parents. In other cases, it came from following Christian principles.

Going to church can cause friction with parents, especially for single returnees. Some parents perceive time in church as time taken from them. Others are alarmed that their dear children (especially daughters) want to travel for an hour to some unknown part of the city to a church that is not approved by the government. They wonder, "Who are these people? Are they honest? Will they take advantage of my daughter?"

Some returnees live with their parents for the first time in years, following undergraduate study in another Chinese city and then postgraduate study abroad. One returnee posted a picture of her bedroom on WeChat. It looked like the room of a young teenager; maybe her parents still see her like that. Visiting her home, I wondered if *she* still felt like a teenager in that environment.

Other returnees give up meeting with Christians because their parents, or much-loved grandparents, follow Buddhism and are fearful of the consequences of having Christians in the family.

The Christians' desire to be with their *church* family is linked with their view of God as their ultimate Father, mentioned earlier. Returnees must work out ways of putting God first while still honoring their parents. Church friends who have been through the same problems can provide vital support. Their welcome can be instrumental in cases where parents join the church family themselves and become believers.

Marriage relationships

The divorce rate has increased greatly in China, from 0.4 percent in 1985 to 3.9 percent in 2015. This is still very low compared to many countries. There is a huge difference between the rates in urban and rural areas, however. Divorce in Beijing, for example, has been cited as 40 percent.[82] Reasons suggested include children born under the one-child policy being unable to sustain relationships; the introduction of laws allowing couples to divorce cheaply in one day; the changing situation of urban women; and social media making having an affair easier. This is the context within which five returnees told me that following biblical teaching on marriage, prayer, and forgiveness had protected them from divorce.

The new view embraced by Changlan and Fuyin that their spouse, and marriage itself, were not to be treated casually, or given up lightly, related to their understanding that these are gifts from God. The transformation experienced by Changlan and Luli, from seeing marriage as about them being loved, to seeing it as about mutual love and sacrificial concern for the other, runs counter to a society that increasingly seeks divorce quickly.

Some years ago a baptized Chinese returnee friend phoned to say that he was considering divorcing his wife. He was already working in a different city

---

82   Figures in this paragraph are from the Chinese Ministry of Civil Affairs, according to Yiying Fan, "'Divorced Yet?'—Why China Has a Soaring Divorce Rate," *What's on Weibo* website, July 16, 2015, http://www.whatsonweibo.com/divorced-yet-why-china-has-a-soaring-divorce-rate/.

than the family home. I listened, prayed, and counseled him to rethink. His best friend, not a Christian, was encouraging him to divorce—telling him he could easily find someone else. God answered my prayer: my friend stayed with his wife, and years later they both bear testimony to God's goodness. But at the time, most voices around him were telling him only to think of himself.

Married Christians in my study described a concern to see their spouse's point of view and to forgive, which was related to a self-concept that included seeing *themselves* as forgiven by God. Fuyin linked God's forgiveness "streaming down" on her to her own ability to forgive her father. And rather than focusing on her husband's shortcomings, she now saw how kind he had been over the years.

These people sought help from the Bible about marriage, prayed together, heard about it in sermons, and discussed it with other Christian couples. Changlan told me how important church friends were when he and his girlfriend (now wife) were living in different cities and he was thinking of breaking off the relationship. The church community encouraged him to work at it. Later they were helped by a church marriage course. Xue was strengthened, through strong church friendships with others who shared her values, to resist her parents' attempts to marry her to a non-Christian man.

Individuals whose spouses aren't Christians face much greater challenges. Chenhong's wife mocked him, criticized his desire to attend church, and made it awkward for him to do so. Other spouses weren't that critical, but had other things they wanted to do on Sundays.

Parenthood

A study of Taiwanese Christian parents in California revealed how they changed after becoming Christians. They saw Christ as head of the family and their children as gifts from God. They saw themselves as stewards charged with the responsibility of caring for their children and bringing out their individual God-given personalities, interests, and abilities. One father described his new belief that God is both just *and* loving, contrasting it with his earlier Confucian model of fatherhood. That model emphasized justice and the child's obedience and duty to parents, but did not emphasize showing children love. Parents now recognized their children as "separate and autonomous individuals who belong to God."[83] The nature of the family bond changed.

Three female returnees in my study later became involved in Christian education. One started an international section in a private school; her classes are run on Christian principles and the teachers are Christians. Another supports her husband in his role as headmaster of a school linked with a house church. The third trains churches in parenting and family matters. I know other female returnees who have stopped work, or found ways of working reduced hours (not that easy in China) in order to care for their children themselves rather than

---

83 Carolyn Chen, "From Filial Piety to Religious Piety: Evangelical Christianity Reconstructing Taiwanese Immigrant Families in the United States," *International Migration Review* 40, no. 3 (2006): 573–602, specifically 593.

rely on grandparents or an *āyí* (阿姨), a woman paid to care for children and do some housework.

Empathy and tolerance

Interviewees stated that they were now better at seeing things from other people's perspectives. They were more tolerant and less likely to make snap judgments of people. This smoothed family and work relationships.

Ruolan said her new desire and ability to get along well with colleagues came from a realization that other people are not "enemies" to be overcome. She understands the pressures they face better now.

Scholars have found that the overseas study experience itself helps returnees socially upon their return.[84] Coping and succeeding in a foreign context, in a foreign language, with different academic methods and diverse opinions, can bring confidence and skills that remain after return.

Biblical teaching and experience of Christian community abroad are very significant too. Ruolan was adamant that God was the prime mover behind her change. She linked her increased empathy and tolerance with her new sense of her own sin, selfishness, and limitations. Reading the Bible helped her understand this. I think that being a Christian and her experience abroad both influenced the way she saw herself and others. Her church experience in China helped her maintain this confident outlook toward others by reinforcing her identity as a child of God. She was learning to love others rather than to think of them as competitors. This is hugely important in China, where the education system emphasizes competition.

Understanding how the biblical big picture relates to us, knowing what Christ has done and what it means to be a child of God, having close relationships with other Christians—these are essential if returnees are to become rooted in Christ and produce fruit, in China or wherever they go. Let's look at how we can help.

---

84   Qing Gu, Michele Schweisfurth, and Christopher Day, "Learning and Growing in a 'Foreign' Context: Intercultural Experiences of International Students," *Compare* 40, no. 1 (2010): 7–23.

PART 5
The Implications

10 So How Can We Help?

> Then Jesus came to them and said, "All authority in heaven and on earth has been given to me. Therefore go and make disciples of all nations, baptizing them in the name of the Father and of the Son and of the Holy Spirit, and teaching them to obey everything I have commanded you."
>
> Matthew 28:18–20

After returning to China, Yue gradually became a church leader. Xiaodan and her husband started a church. Fuyin and her husband went to seminary. Yet so many fall away. Some become isolated from Christian believers; some pursue status or money; some fear shaming their parents; some fear the authorities. And as one missiologist has observed, "Not all conversions to Christianity represent conversions to Christ."[85] Some love the love of Christians, but don't see beyond that; they don't see their own sin and shame and what Christ has done for them.

Here are some suggestions for how we can help people become rooted in Christ before they return. Some are with us for years while others return to China after just a few months, so I realize this won't all be possible every time. But part of it will be.

Think China

People from different cultures and contexts have different ways of thinking. That applies to all of us, wherever we are from. People from China return to somewhere very different than their place of study overseas. We need to have that in mind from day one. We don't all need to be experts on Chinese culture, but we can read a little, and maybe even visit China.

Chinese students, of course, know a lot about China! They can help us understand the Chinese family and society. We just need to ask good questions. One exception, though: Unless they are mature Christians, they won't know much about the nature of the church in China. We may need to find others to help us, and them, understand that.

---

85   Brian Stanley, "Conversion to Christianity: The Colonization of the Mind?" *International Review of Mission* 92, no. 366 (2003): 315–31, specifically 326.

As we are leading Bible studies we can ask questions that encourage students to apply what they are learning to the Chinese context. Rather than using a standard evangelistic Bible study written for people in our country, we might choose one with questions that relate to China.[86] Then they are less likely to see the study as a mere cultural experience, relevant only for the time they are in the host country.

We can involve mainland Chinese Christians in our ministry; they might identify misunderstandings or explain things that puzzle us. Weekend conferences and Bible camps—run by Chinese Christians, in Mandarin, prepared especially for Chinese students—can be turning points.

Introduce God's Big Picture[87]

Think of Jesus walking with the two disciples on the road to Emmaus (Luke 24:13–32), or Philip riding in the Ethiopian official's chariot on the road to Gaza (Acts 8:26–38). They both explained the big picture: they related the Old Testament to Jesus; they related it to the individuals they were with.

I'm not saying it's always necessary to *start* with a Bible overview, just that it's important to do so at some point. Helping people grasp the big picture of the whole Bible, rather than just one Gospel, is worthwhile. It may be hard, if students are only in our country for a year or less, but even a brief overview can help. We see our creator God's concern for humanity. We see him building his kingdom.

We need the whole Bible trajectory, from Genesis to Revelation, to show that the biblical story is about a people from all nations—including China. Every believer needs to know the history of God's people, *their* people. Today's China has a rich history and a powerful future, according to Xi Jinping's Chinese Dream. Yet the biblical perspective offers a compelling master story that can stand up to and even illuminate the Chinese story. God's people in the Bible are our spiritual ancestors; Chinese Christians need to know who they are descended from!

As we reflect on the story of Israel and the early church, we make more sense of our own struggles. The story of God's people becomes our story too and helps us keep going. Acquiring this big picture takes time, of course, but we can help new believers start the process.

Knowing about the history of the church in China can encourage them too. Websites provide stories and information about their Chinese Christian forebears, people like John Sung (Sung Shangjie) and Xi Shengmo.[88] Sung was a returnee too. He had a PhD in chemistry but gave his life to winning souls for

---

86 The Bible studies from Mark's Gospel found on the Sea Turtles website are good examples: https://www.seaturtles.org.uk/bible-studies/.

87 This is the name of a book written by Vaughan Roberts (InterVarsity Press, 2009). It has been translated into Chinese. Websites for purchasing it are shown on the resources page of the Sea Turtles website: www.seaturtles.org.uk.

88 For example, the online Biographical Dictionary of Chinese Christianity: http://www.bdc-conline.net/en/.

Christ. Xi was a Confucian scholar and opium addict. He turned to Christ, gave up opium, and helped many others do the same.

Some people are reluctant to read the Old Testament because they think the Old Testament God was not good and kind, that he was somehow replaced by the loving, kind Jesus. Telling the story of God's relationship with Israel—his promises, patience, and faithfulness despite Israel's unfaithfulness—dispels such misunderstandings.

Baozhai had a concept of God as Father and some idea of the Spirit, but very little understanding of the Son. She needed to know all three. She lacked an understanding of human sin and the need for reconciliation with God. Some exposure to the Old Testament and the prophecies about Christ, linked to a gospel narrative of Christ's teaching about sin and his death and resurrection, would have helped her.

She could well have benefited from an honor-shame perspective too. I'm currently using *The Creator King*, a six-step overview by Jackson Wu,[89] to see if people find it helpful. It provides a whole-Bible big picture and also brings out major elements that resonate strongly with Chinese culture but often get left out of gospel presentations. I am hoping the focus on shame and honor will help people understand sin better. The focus on God's family may also help them appreciate the importance of the community aspect of Christian life.

Help Them Know (and Live) Who They Are

Understanding our own sin and shame, and just how much Christ has done for us, is essential for knowing what it is to be a child of God. People like Xiaodan and Xue know their own sin and shortcomings *and* they know God as a loving Father. They know they have a new identity in Christ; whatever has happened, and will happen, they are his loved child. They also know they have a new purpose and that fulfilling that purpose will not always be easy.

Sharing a vision, instilling a mission

God has given his children the ministry and message of reconciliation; we are to be Christ's ambassadors (2 Cor 5:18–20). What an amazing privilege and responsibility!

A Chinese colleague in the US changed his approach a couple of years ago: he started focusing on sharing this mission and vision with new Chinese student believers. They are commissioned to return to China as Christ's ambassadors. If possible, they go in pairs or small groups to the same cities. These *missionaries* are prayed for and people stay in touch with them. My colleague has been to visit and encourage them. They are bearing fruit.

Disciples and disciple-makers—Not consumers

Another experienced student worker wrote that when international student ministry "is stuck in 'service land,' students become customers or, even worse,

---

89   http://www.patheos.com/blogs/jacksonwu/2015/05/06/introducing-the-creator-king/.

mere consumers of our goods."[90] I think he was right on target. We need to make disciples—and disciple-makers—not consumers of our noble services.

Consumers get used to having everything done for them; they get used to being fed, from both the kitchen and the pulpit. There's no effort; they get used to the attention and generosity, the hospitality, the rides to church. But it's not like that when they get home. People in China don't have time to do all that for them. One returnee put it like this:

> Churches abroad gave us five-star service; we got used to real VIP treatment. That was great. Thank you. But tell the Chinese students: "TIC! This Is China. Real life in China is tough. And you are not a student anymore. You cannot expect to be nurtured as you were abroad. Take every chance overseas to learn how to feed yourself from God's Word."

We'll come back to this last point in the section below regarding living under a new authority.

Equipping for service

Students need to serve while they are overseas. This might take place in the context of a small group or at church: serving coffee, cooking, cleaning, welcoming, playing music, leading a Bible study, contributing ideas for an evangelistic course, translating materials—all sorts of things, depending on the person and the stage of his or her Christian walk.

It is wonderful to see a previously wary seeker who is now believing and joyfully reaching out to new international arrivals. As one of our church cooks, I really enjoyed handing over the lead to a Chinese man who makes much tastier Chinese food than I do. It wasn't just the food I enjoyed, but seeing a previously reserved man getting involved—enjoying serving and helping others serve.

Sharing tasks and projects helps people learn patience and humility. It also provides opportunities to relate closely with people outside one's blood family, which can be a useful experience for people from a culture in which families typically only had one child and in which close relationships with people beyond the family and workplace are unusual.

We can also open people's eyes to see how their gifts, abilities, education, and career might serve God. This can be done through Bible studies on work or on Bible characters—Daniel, Joseph, and Naaman's servant girl come to mind. It can also be done by introducing individuals to Christians in their field or profession who actively serve God through their work: engineers, teachers, lawyers, academics, businesspeople. There may be a related Christian conference they could go to or a network they could join.

Christian returnees can make great contributions to society. What starts small—for example, one couple working with people with leprosy or another teaching migrant children—can change attitudes, behavior, and even social policy.

---

90   Christopher Sneller, "Getting Unstuck from Service Land: From Service-oriented Ministries to Disciple-making Movements," *Mission Frontiers* 38, no. 4 (2016): 18–21.

Helping them share Christ

It's good for Chinese believers to practise sharing their testimony; then we can pray for them as they relate to classmates, roommates, and family. We can look out for vacation outreach activities. In the UK, for example, cities such as Edinburgh, Oxford, and Cambridge host outreaches to the many language students who flock there for short courses in the summer. These provide new believers with training, a chance to join a team, and great experience.

Those with a few months between finishing their studies and the expiration of their visa may be able to volunteer with their church, using their cross-cultural experience to support outreach. Some Chinese mission agencies have volunteer programs that provide opportunities for new believers to take part in campus outreach, receive Bible teaching in Chinese, and serve in practical ways.

Other ministries offer an avenue for Christian international students to stay for another whole year after completing their degrees; as volunteers, they receive training and great opportunities to serve and share the gospel. I can think of several Chinese people who have stayed to serve in these ways, and they have all gone on to contribute significantly in churches in China or in helping other returnees settle into church.

If visa regulations allow, it may also be possible to enroll for training in urban mission. Such an experience in, say Chicago or Sydney, could prepare a new believer to contribute in China's big cities. Even if such in-depth training isn't feasible, volunteering once a week with a project in their host city may be.

Teaching about suffering and spiritual warfare

Jesus said that loyalty to him will involve self-denial and even suffering. One area of potential conflict is the family. Addressing this subject in Matthew 10:34–37, Jesus spoke these tough words: "I did not come to bring peace, but a sword" (v. 34). Chinese students need to be helped to think through the implications of verse 37: "Anyone who loves their father or mother more than me is not worthy of me."

I help run retreats for new believers preparing to return home. We always have a session on the spiritual battle. By that I mean that we tell people about the devil and his methods as depicted in the Bible and about Jesus' victory over the devil; and we discuss what can help us in the battle. This is kinder than leaving the impression, which some take home, that being a Christian means they will have no more problems and everything will go their way.

In Ephesians 6:10–20, Paul explains that there are evil forces beyond the human. One Chinese student whose parents objected to her faith was so relieved to read that we "do not wrestle against flesh and blood"; she loves her parents and doesn't want to see *them* as the enemy.

Help Them Live under a Different Authority

But we don't want to create dependence on our teaching; returnees need to be dependent on God and his Word, the Bible.

Living from the Bible

My returnee friend sent this message to Chinese studying abroad: "Take every chance overseas to learn how to feed yourself from God's Word." He's not the only one to say that. Chinese ministers have told me: "These returnees don't know how to read the Bible; please teach them."

People need to know how to read the Bible without depending on notes. Inductive Bible study methods can be demonstrated. Some international student workers use an approach that asks a simple set of questions and encourages the readers to take ownership of the study, apply the questions to their own lives, obey or trust what God tells them in the passage, and share what they have learned—right from the first evangelistic study.[91] We may feel we are losing control if we teach less; but if students are learning to read, pray, and trust God's Word, rather than ours, this may be the greatest gift we can share.

The students we spend time with will be as interested in what we do as what we say. It's quite a challenge to me to think that they will be watching whether or not I live out what we discuss during the study. Sharing how we pray, how we make decisions, what we do when things go wrong—modeling—is important too!

Identifying the old authorities

Now that God is in the new believer's life, he is the ultimate authority. People will benefit from identifying the main authority in their life previously. Was it their parents? Was it their boss? Or were they the proud controller of their own destiny? They need to pray and prepare how they will relate to those people and how they will ensure they allow God his rightful place. Certain behavior may need to change, sooner rather than later. They may need someone to hold them accountable—and that might be you or it might be a Chinese Christian friend. Prayer triplets can be very helpful: maybe three people who will be returning to China about the same time.

Help Them Adopt God's Values

In order to please God we need to know what he wants, what matters to him most—in other words, to bring our values in line with his. As we seek to live under God's authority, obeying his Word and Spirit, we become better able "to test and approve what God's will is" (Rom 12:2).

Jesus knew what the rich young man's core value, or "object of worship," was. It was his wealth. And Jesus challenged him about it (Matt 19:16–22).

---

91   The July/August 2016 issue of *Mission Frontiers* was dedicated to international students and included two articles on Discovery Bible Study, one by Rich Mendola and one by Derrah Jackson, https://www.missionfrontiers.org/pdfs/2016_38–4_MF.pdf.

There's a place for us challenging each other too—with prayer and humility, of course. That includes challenging our new Christian Chinese brothers and sisters. As Proverbs 27:17 says, "Iron sharpens iron."

We need to prove we are trustworthy if we are going to do that. If we have a good relationship, we can help new believers look back over their lives and understand the values that drove them in the past. We can help them reflect on what motivated their decisions in the past, what made them happy, what was really difficult, how they spent their time. This will give them clues as to what their core values were. Some of those will need to change to come in line with God's values.

Returnees also need to look forward and decide how they are going to respond to the more challenging aspects of Chinese life and the values underlying them: ancestor worship, idol worship, folk religions, pursuing status and wealth, pressure to marry by a certain age, unethical business practices. Just as Paul "looked carefully" at the Athenians' "objects of worship," so returnees need to consider, before they return, which Chinese values are going to conflict with God's values and which are in line with them. Then they can pray and plan how to respond. Case studies can be very helpful; maybe the stories in this book could provide a few.

However, their response needs to go beyond reading and talking and also involve action. What, for example, can they do *now*, while still overseas, to be good stewards of the time, money, and skills God has given them? What about taking some time—and money—to serve on a missions outreach or go on a weekend retreat to prepare for their return? If they "can't afford" the time or money to do it now, will they when they get back to China? Maybe not.

We can take students along to things that we're doing. This is part of modeling what it means to adopt God's values. I once took a Chinese friend to a weekend missions conference; some of the sessions were about China, and some of those speakers weren't Chinese. My friend was bowled over that these people had given up so much to go and live in a foreign country, her country, because they wanted her people to know Jesus—and all these other foreigners were praying for them all!

Another way for us to model living according to God's values is to invite students to live in our home. It's challenging, since they will see our failures. But that can be part of the discipleship—for all of us.

Build a Bridge to Church Family in China

All sorts of obstacles get in the way of returnees becoming part of the church family in China. Some arise because life is different back home. Others arise because we don't adequately convey the nature and importance of God's family, the church.

Experiencing Christianity as Chinese before return
Chinese students need to get used to reading the Bible and praying in Chinese. I witnessed a situation in which an articulate returnee who was used to praying

in English was unable to pray, when asked to, in a small group in Shanghai. She was simply unfamiliar with Chinese Christian terminology.

Those of us in English-speaking churches need to help students experience church and Christianity as Chinese *while abroad*. It makes a huge difference. Being with mainland Chinese Christians isn't just helpful for language reasons, but also for the shared cultural experiences: seeing other Chinese being God's family for each other, and hearing the Bible explained in a way that relates to China and Chinese concerns. Then they can know and *feel* that the Christian story is also a Chinese story. Church is less likely to be a foreign cultural experience easily left behind in a busy life back home.

This doesn't mean that all Chinese students abroad should go to Chinese churches and the rest of us have nothing to offer. Far from it! But some exposure is very helpful. This might be in a Chinese church, but it could also be in an English-speaking church that has a Mandarin-speaking fellowship or in a Mandarin-speaking campus fellowship. It could be in a weekly mainland Chinese-led Bible study, an occasional Chinese-language Bible camp, or simply meeting to pray with a Chinese Christian friend.

In the US and UK, there are Chinese-language preparatory retreats. These offer the chance to discuss Bible-based responses to the opportunities and challenges of Christian life in China, to learn about the Chinese church, and to network with others who will be returning at the same time.

Teaching about church

There is a big difference between a social activity and the Christian family. New Chinese believers need to understand that. The implications—and the wonder—of being part of the body of Christ need to be explored. They need to know what the Bible says about what (and who) the church is and what it is for: the people of God, the bride of Christ, the adopted children of God, and a light to others. The plural nature of many such descriptions also highlights that Christians need each other.

It is important to discuss potential difficulties of church life too. Chinese students can be oblivious to problems in churches, or unaware of the sacrifice and hard work that goes into running a church and building relationships that honor God. Paul has plenty to say about that in 1 Corinthians and 1 Timothy; lack of love, seeking to uphold one's own "rights" to the detriment of the gospel, and knowing when to submit are all mentioned.

Committing to church

Xiaodan, Xue, Changlan, and others understood that they had not just been reborn for a private relationship with God and that being a Christian is not something to be done alone. They searched out fellowship immediately upon their return, and soon thereafter they were serving in church small groups or setting up a group, such as a young marrieds' group or a returnees' gathering.

One committed returnee Christian deliberately rented an apartment near a good church; another chose work that fit the location and service times of the church he had already identified. Being part of their church communities has strengthened their faith and ability to help others. Qingzhao managed to negotiate time off work on Sundays so she could take part in church. Some returnees continue working on Sunday, but join a midweek fellowship.

Identifying false teaching

Jesus warned his disciples, "Many will come in my name, claiming, 'I am the Messiah,' and will deceive many" (Matt 24:5). We don't need to scare returnees, but we can help them identify gospel essentials and warning signs that something may not be right. Such signs could include the behavior and lifestyle of preachers being different than what they preach; the suggestion that a particular church is the only good one; a church teaching from a version of the Bible that only they use; an overemphasis on praying for personal prosperity or success in business; an insufficient view of Jesus or needing something in addition to Jesus. Jeremiah 23, Matthew 7, and significant portions of Paul's letters address false teaching.

Some Chinese scholars recommend a return to Confucianism as a way of helping China build moral values. Others look to Christianity and the Bible for the same reason. Some of these proponents come to faith in Christ as Savior, but others are only interested in Christianity as a philosophy. When people profess faith, we need to be sure it is because they believe the gospel is *true* and not merely *useful*.

Deciding what to look for in a church

Prayer for returnees to have spiritual discernment, wisdom, and humility is important. Acts 2:42 provides a good starting point for discussion in regard to evaluating churches. The ID Course[92] recommends that returnees should consider the following: is the Word of God central in this church (2 Tim 3:14–17)? Would the returnee be able to respect and submit to the leadership (because the leaders are good shepherds who demonstrate the characteristics listed in 1 Pet 5:1–3)? Does this church share the gospel with those outside the church (e.g., 1 Thess 1:8)? What opportunities are there to serve God in this church (e.g., Rom 12:4–8)? While admitting that love can look different in different cultural contexts, I would add "Do they love each other here (John 13:34,35)?"

Sadly, many returnees are disappointed or critical because they are unable to find a church just like the one they attended abroad. They need to be forewarned that churches will seem different, but that doesn't necessarily make them inadequate. A little prior preparation and experience abroad can help them discern whether differences are central to the gospel or merely peripheral—and whether to join a church or to keep looking.

It can be helpful for returnees to visit a few other churches while they are abroad and discuss what they observed. It is also useful for those who have only known English-speaking churches to visit Chinese churches abroad and experience worship in Chinese. Though this has to do with language, it also has to do with identity and style.

---

92 The ID (or International Discipleship) Course is a series of studies for international students developed by Friends International.

I recently attended a retreat for Chinese new Christians in the UK, and I watched as the participants sang together. The majority were used to English-speaking churches, so this was the first time they had sung worship songs in Chinese and in a different style. I could sense their hesitancy and discomfort. Afterward, several asked if we could sing in English instead of Chinese! We pointed out that they were having a foretaste of church culture shock. That insight helped them.

Encouraging prayer about existing relationships

Earlier chapters revealed how returnees learned new ways of relating to parents and others. Changlan, for example, found ways of *honoring* his parents without *obeying* them, if doing so would mean compromising his relationship with Jesus. Helping new believers reflect and pray about key relationships before they return is important. What individuals will be most affected by the changes in their lives? What objections might this people have to their faith? What does the Bible say about these things? What is the most helpful way of introducing these individuals to Christ? How will they respond if their much-loved parents reject the gospel?

Making contacts in advance of return

Jesus warned about "life's worries, riches and pleasures" (Luke 8:14). Since Chinese life is particularly busy and full of these kinds of distractions, it is extremely helpful if returnees are introduced to Christians in their city before their return. Increasingly there are returnees who have already been through the reverse culture shock, the joys and challenges, the church hunt. Knowing such a person can make a huge difference. And even if there are no other returnees, having a contact in a church greatly increases the likelihood that a returnee will actually *go*.

Large international student ministries and Chinese mission agencies outside China are increasingly able to point Christian returnees[93] and their overseas helpers to Christian contacts in China—not everywhere, but certainly in the larger cities. Some cities also have returnee fellowships that support new returnees through the initial difficulties and in finding a church.

Staying in touch

Don't underestimate the importance of staying in touch with your friends after they return. You may be the only person encouraging them and praying for them to settle into a church. Reading the Bible and praying with you via Skype or FaceTime could be what keeps them going.

I've heard Western Christians talk about returnees being "handed over" to the church in China. They imagined returnees just walking into a church and meeting mature believers who would immediately befriend and disciple them; their own role was over. It just isn't like that. Even when returnees connect with a Christian who can take them to church, it doesn't necessarily mean that person

---

93   Security concerns and limited resources mean that it is not so easy to link those who are interested in joining a Bible study group but have not made a commitment to Christ.

will have the time or experience to disciple them, or know them well enough to follow up when they don't go to church. Our efforts to stay in regular contact can make all the difference, until they are really established in fellowship— maybe not forever, but at least for a few months.

Ways We Can Help Ourselves

Identify misunderstandings

We should expect misunderstandings, especially if we aren't from mainland China or don't speak Chinese. We may misunderstand a Chinese person's reaction to the Bible or to us, and they may misinterpret what they see or hear.

We need to ask good questions in order to help students express what they think without feeling they must give the "right" answer. Also, just because we have "covered" a topic doesn't mean the other person has either understood or assented. I'm sure I didn't learn what I know now in a logical progression! I have had to revisit passages and issues in the Bible over the years. Why should international students be different? We need to be ready to diverge from planned courses and go over old ground in a different way.

Don't go it alone: Work in partnership

Reading all this may have left you thinking, "I can't do all that!" You're right. You can't, and neither can I. We need help from our brothers and sisters: in our own church, in international student ministries, in Chinese churches and missions. And that's fine. We don't want to replicate ourselves or create dependency on ourselves. God has made us each part of his body, an international body, with different things to offer.[94]

A mainland Chinese Christian may be able to identify what another mainland Chinese thinks when a non-Chinese cannot. Attending an evangelistic or discipling camp run by a Chinese mission, in Chinese, can lead to a huge step forward in someone's understanding.

We need to be ready to identify our weaknesses and work in partnership with others, especially Chinese Christians.

Find out what's available

People may be available to talk things through with you. They may be able to provide training for you and others in your church. Or they may know of a resource or a retreat that might be great for your Chinese friend.

If you don't know where to turn for help, you could contact OMF's Diaspora Returnee Ministries[95] or an international student ministry. In North America, various agencies could help; the website of ACMI (the Association of

---

94   For more on partnership, including my article, "Functioning as the Body to Build the Body," see *ChinaSource Quarterlies* 18, no. 3 (2016), https://www.chinasource.org/resource-library/chinasource-quarterlies/a-call-to-partnership-in-chinese-returnee-ministry.

95   https://omf.org/asia/diaspora/.

Christians Ministering among Internationals) is a good starting point.[96] In the UK, there is Friends International (and their website with lots of resources)[97] or the Chinese Overseas Christian Mission (COCM).[98] In Australia, you could start by looking at ThrivingTurtles.org. In New Zealand, you could look up ISMNZ.[99]

And finally . . . think return from day one—what this book is about!

---

96   https://www.acmi-ism.org/.
97   https://friendsinternational.uk/resources/downloadable-resources.
98   https://www.cocm.org.uk/.
99   www.ismnz.org.nz/.

11 Closing Encouragement

> *After this I looked, and there before me was a great multitude that no one could count, from every nation, tribe, people and language, standing before the throne and before the Lamb. They were wearing white robes and were holding palm branches in their hands. And they cried out in a loud voice: "Salvation belongs to our God, who sits on the throne, and to the Lamb."*

Revelation 7:9,10

Song Shangjie (John Sung) was an earlier returnee. After his return from the US to China, in 1927, he dedicated his life to preaching the gospel. Thousands in China and Southeast Asia came to believe in Christ through Song's work. The potential of new Christian returnees is huge, whether God uses them to reach thousands, like Song, or in less dramatic ways. Many do fall away, but, as this book shows, there is so much we can do to reduce that number.

A quotation from Song helps explain something that has been on my mind while writing: "Man's works do not even come close to the works of the Holy Spirit. If the Holy Spirit does not work, all the efforts of man will come to naught."[100]

This book was written to help *people* help other people know, and keep following, Jesus Christ. There are many illustrations of what people have done or not done and suggestions of what we might do to help each other. Yet, as Song points out, our work is nothing if the Holy Spirit is not at work. I have not written much about the Spirit, but I want readers to know that I acknowledge that our efforts are nothing without him. Indeed, what a relief that he is in charge.

Nor have I said much about prayer. Of course, prayer must be central to all we do. Indeed, answers to prayer and the many encouragements from seeing God at work could form another book. James Hudson Taylor, the founder of the China Inland Mission, is a powerful example. His son Howard said of him:,

---

100 Levi (Compiler), *The Diary of John Sung: Extracts from his Journals and Notes* (Armour Publishing, Singapore, 2012), 66.

""He prayed about things as if everything depended upon the praying ... but he worked also, as if everything depended on his working."[101]

Finally, I have a message to pass on. It's a message to you, from returnees. I often ask people who have returned to China if they have a message for Christians overseas who serve international students, Chinese students. It's generally a similar response: "thank you." They want to thank *you*.

One returnee said this when asked what advice she had for Christians abroad who meet Chinese students:

> They do a good job. Try to walk into the heart of Chinese students. I believe any of the students has a story of her life. The story means the need, the trigger, that makes her think and look for the belief. That could be something that happened, happy or unhappy, in her life earlier or recently, emotionally or realistically. There must be something there that, in her heart, grows hardly, that you can find and then talk with her to find herself, what she needs, what she worries or what she's thirsty about.

She was not suggesting we all become psychoanalysts; she was simply suggesting we get to know people and care for them. Personal understanding is needed to win someone's trust; then, when we have that, she says, people will be willing to look at God's words for their own lives:

> When you know what is her need, she will go to you to find the answer from there [i.e., from the Bible].

As we get to know each other, students will see how the Bible relates to *our* lives, and then be better able to relate it to their own lives. We can help them see how the Bible's history, good news, and promises are their history and future too. We can help them identify what it means for them personally to be a loved child of God.

Sometimes this will be pure joy; at other times it will take much effort. It is always a privilege. It's encouraging to remember that we are part of a chain of people whom God chooses to bring into other's lives, and most encouraging that God himself oversees everything. "I planted the seed, Apollos watered it, but God has been making it grow" (1 Cor 3:6).

---

101   A.J. Broomhall. *Hudson Taylor and China's Open Century, Book Six: Assault on the Nine* (London, Hodder and Stoughton and Overseas Missionary Fellowship, 1988), 194.

Suggestions for Further Reading

This is a short list. Further suggestions can be found within these books.

Christianity in China

See the ChinaSource website (http://www.chsource.org/) for up-to-date information and articles written by Chinese church leaders and translated into English.

The Spirit of China: The Roots of Faith in Twenty-first Century China, David Burnett, Monarch, 2008; traces the wider religious history, not only Christianity.

Surviving the State, Remaking the Church: A Sociological Portrait of Christians in Mainland China, Li Ma and Jin Li, Pickwick, 2017; covers the period from 1949 to 2017, providing glimpses into the lives of individual Christians to throw light on the church in China today

China's Urban Christians: A Light That Cannot Be Hidden, Brent Fulton, Pickwick, 2015; considers how the Chinese church is responding to the massive changes brought about by China's urbanization.

The Coming Chinese Church, Paul Golf, Monarch, 2013.

God Is Red: The Secret Story of How Christianity Survived and Flourished in Communist China, Liao Yiwu, HarperOne, 2012.

The Chinese Puzzle, Mike Falkenstine, Xulon, 2008.

China's Christian Millions: The Costly Revival (revised edition), Tony Lambert, Monarch, 2006.

Jesus in Beijing, David Aikman, Monarch, 2006.

Biographical Dictionary of Chinese Christianity (www.bdcconline.net); database of short biographies of influential Christians in China, from about 1800 to 1950.

History

China: A History, John Keay, HarperPress, 2008; covers three thousand years.

The Chinese Century: A Photographic History, Jonathan Spence and Annping Chen, HarperCollins, 1996.

Son of the Revolution, Liang Heng and Judith Shapiro, Fontana, 1983; autobiography of Liang Heng, who was born in 1954.

Moving the Mountain, Li Lu, Macmillan, 1990; Li was a child during the Cultural Revolution and a student during the 1989 Tiananmen protest.

A Chinese Life, Li Kunwu and Philippe Otie, SelfMadeHero, 2012; autobiography written in graphic novel form.

Other

The ChinaSource website (http://www.chinasource.org/) also provides ZGBriefs, a weekly compilation of China-related news items.

Wish Lanterns: Young Lives in New China, Alec Ash, Picador, 2016.

The Geography of Thought: How Asians and Westerners Think Differently . . . and Why, Richard E. Nisbett, Nicholas Brealey Publishing, 2005.

Age of Ambition: Chasing Fortune, Truth, and Faith in the New China, Evan Osnos, The Bodley Head, 2014.

Only Hope: Coming of Age Under China's One-Child Policy, Vanessa Fong, Stanford University Press, 2004.

Crossing Cultures with Jesus: Sharing Good News with Sensitivity and Grace, Katie J. Rawson, InterVarsity Press, 2015.

For an extensive reading list and reviews of books, see the Global China Center website (http://www.globalchinacenter.org/resources/recommended-reading/).